C000067192

125 YEARS OF
DURHAM HIGH SCHOOL *for* GIRLS

A Birthday Celebration

125 YEARS OF
DURHAM HIGH SCHOOL *for* GIRLS

A Birthday Celebration

THIRD MILLENNIUM
PUBLISHING, LONDON

125 years of Durham High School for Girls: A Birthday Celebration
© 2009 Durham High School for Girls and Third Millennium Publishing Limited

First published in 2009 by
Third Millennium Publishing Limited,
a subsidiary of Third Millennium Information Limited.

2–5 Benjamin Street
London
United Kingdom
EC1M 5QL
www.tmiltd.com

ISBN : 978 1 906507 07 7
All rights reserved.

No part of this publication may be reproduced or transmitted
in any form or by any means, electronic or mechanical,
including photocopying, recording or any storage or retrieval
system, without permission in writing from the publisher.

British Library Cataloguing in Publication Data
A CIP catalogue record for this book is available from the British Library

Design: Matthew Wilson
Production: Bonnie Murray

Reprographics and Printing by Butler Tanner and Dennis

Contents

Foreword

To have survived for 125 years is no small achievement. To have not merely survived, but flourished, and through such momentous changes in the world around, suggests a touch of greatness. This book is a record of that achievement: and it may be that, as readers follow the story which unfolds here, they will recognise that here indeed is a 'great' school. Great in the dedication of its successive Heads and teaching staff, great in the sequence of Chairmen and Governors and their colleagues who have steered it; great in the sense of community nourished here from the earliest days, often through difficult times, great alike in the quality of its academic work and of the breadth of wider interests offered and fostered. And great above all in the Christian vision which founded it and the strong Christian sense of service which throughout these 125 years has faithfully carried forward the school's life.

At a time when faith schools are under closer and more rigorous – even sceptical – scrutiny than perhaps ever before, here is a record to present with conviction and joy. For here is a story of the best kind of Christian education, rooted in faith but always outward-looking, humane, generous, world-engaging, requiring of its students and staff members alike the very best they can be, not for ambition's sake but for the greater good of the world in which the school is set. And so I recommend this book as a record of how to 'do it well', to all those who care not only about girls' education now and in the future, but that the spiritual dimension of education in England should continue to be cherished and nurtured. For here is a record of blessing. Long may it continue!

Ruth Etchells

Former Principal, St John's College with Cranmer Hall, University of Durham, and sometime Governor of the School

Relaxing in Leazes House gardens, 1960s.

THE BEGINNING

The Beginning

'Daughters should be educated that they might be fit companions for their husbands...'

A well-intentioned pronouncement by the Bishop of Durham in support of a new High School in the city was considered a progressive attitude to the education of girls in 1883. How far we have come!

Now that Durham High School is well into its second century and as we approach our 125th birthday we would like to pause – just briefly since the busy school calendar allows precious few lapses – to reflect on our many achievements to date.

In celebrating all the individuals who have contributed so enthusiastically to our enduring success, which began with eleven long-haired and long-skirted young pioneers in 1884, we have sought to gather together some remembrances which reveal the school's unique character.

Balancing the modern needs of a forward-thinking school with a warm regard for

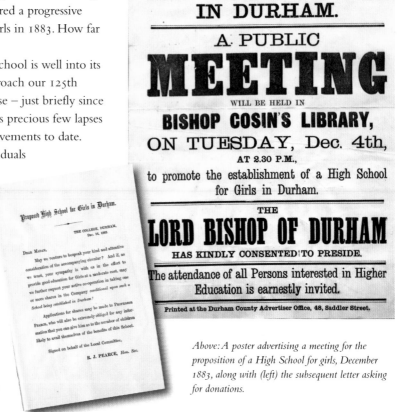

Above: A poster advertising a meeting for the proposition of a High School for girls, December 1883, along with (left) the subsequent letter asking for donations.

PROPOSED HIGH SCHOOL FOR GIRLS IN DURHAM.

Provisional Local Committee.

[List of committee members and proposal text as shown in the reproduced document image]

Left: The full proposal for the School with financial breakdowns included, along with lists of shareholders and provisional committee members.

our past tradition has become central to our philosophy. We have a wealth of history of which to be immensely proud and we are continually striving to maintain links with our rich heritage. As did our predecessors. After all, our second Head Girl became the third headmistress, the seventh headmistress visited the first headmistress, the Head Girl in 1966 came from the 'old' school to plant a tree to mark the beginning of the 'new' school and the 'Jubilee' Head Girl returned to speak at our centenary dinner. There are numerous other life-enhancing ties within our school family – people like to stay connected to us.

Some New Thinking

In the early years of the nineteenth century a sound liberal education might have been sought for the sons of gentlemen, but it was not considered necessary for their daughters. For them, marriage in a state of genteel idleness was the most desirable and socially acceptable occupation. The acquisition of knowledge was deemed irrelevant!

However, even as such thinking began to change and the education of girls became a goal in its own right, there were neither charitable endowments nor public finances available to make it a reality. The task was left to private enterprise and, in 1872, the Girls' Day Schools Company took up the challenge by launching several successful schools.

At about the same time a distinguished group of churchmen and academics formed The Church Schools Company to promote the influence of church teaching on girls' education. Their aim was to create 'a superior education, in accordance with the principles of the Church of England, at a cost sufficient to make the plan self-supporting'.

The Church Schools Company recorded the request for a girls' school in Durham early in December 1883. The proposal was instantly popular, thanks largely to the personal support of Bishop Lightfoot, then Bishop of Durham.

The Bishop had urged the importance of 'the education of wives and mothers of the next generation, in which the good people of Durham were determined not to lag behind'. Though it might not happen that their daughters, like their sons, would be compelled to earn their own livelihood, he believed that girls needed to be prepared for a different future. 'Daughters should be educated that they might be fit companions for their husbands and fit instructors for their children,' he said.

The Doors Opened

It wasn't long before a property had been leased at number 33, Claypath, and the first headmistress, Miss Gray, was appointed. The doors of Durham High School were opened on Tuesday 29 April 1884. Describing the opening *The Durham Advertiser* said: 'We cannot do better than invite such of our readers who have girls to be educated, to follow their example. The high character of the headmistress and the very great care displayed to meeting all the wants of the scholars, combine to open a prospect before this school of a most happy and successful career.'

Despite early problems such as the scarcity of qualified mistresses, the irregularity of school attendance and the inadequacy of rented accommodation with eighteenth-century plumbing, the school grew steadily in numbers and reputation. Clearly it met a need as its first secretary declared to a large assembly in the university lecture room on Palace Green at the first presentation of prizes in July 1885: 'There were many parents anxious to keep their girls at home in the early years of their lives and yet these parents wished their children to be properly prepared for their future.'

A year later the prize giving ceremony was reported in *The Durham Advertiser*: 'The girls all looked exceedingly pretty in their white dresses and coloured sashes and appeared to be in a state of happy excitement.' The chairman said he was happy to report that the success of the school was 'far beyond anything that the early promoters could possibly have imagined. There are now 57 scholars in the school and this examiners' report shows that in every department of the school work was done faithfully, honestly and successfully.'

Top: The Kindergarten in 1892.

Above: An invitation to a prize giving ceremony, 1890.

Opposite: Elizabeth Gray, seen here c.1900, after leaving the School.

Below: 3 South Bailey, the second School building after Claypath was deemed to be too small. This photograph dates from 1892. It's now part of St John's College and named Haughton Hall.

Right: Pupils studying at 3 South Bailey at the beginning of the twentieth century.

University of Durham to the Rescue

The school having grown steadily in numbers, Miss Gray declared the small house on Claypath 'very inadequate for its purpose'. She was obviously relieved when in 1886, with more than 50 pupils, the school moved to number 3 South Bailey – now Haughton Hall, St John's College.

The chief promoter of the school at the time was a professor of mathematics at the University of Durham and his support led to a long and vital connection with the university which continues to this day.

Miss Gray said that the new premises at South Bailey raised the status of the school and gave it '… quiet, commodious and delightful classrooms, with a charming outlook over the river banks'. The school remained there until 12 September 1912.

In the early 1900s school numbers continued to increase and alterations had to be made to accommodate new pupils: the double classroom had to be converted into one large room, 'a great boon for drilling and dancing classes'. The boarders were

moved out of school to number 45 North Bailey. At this time, a new fire escape chute, which was popular with pupils, was installed from the top floor to the garden.

There were continuing problems with accommodation at number 3 South Bailey however: walls needed pointing, there were loose bricks in walls and chimneys, and there were holes in floors. A smoky kitchen range was considered by school staff to be inefficient: 'Its condition causes great waste of coal and adds enormously to the difficulties of housekeeping.'

Girls Must Not 'Spoil Themselves' by Too Much Study

Sound academic standards were established early on by a local committee, ably guided by the

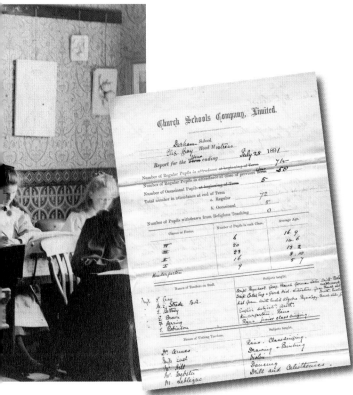

reaching certain standards in education. He feared that pupils' mental powers would be crushed, and children turned out as 'clasped encyclopaedias instead of thinking men and women'. He said he wanted a school where pupils' mental capacities would be drawn out, 'to be ready for the lifelong work of the true educator'.

And at the first Prize Day of the new century, the Dean of Durham feared that the Durham girls might 'spoil themselves by being too eager … and by sitting too long at their studies'. Much of the education in their day ended in the wearing of spectacles, he warned, and he advised the girls to 'study nature as well as their books, and in that way retain their freshness'.

Despite these warnings Miss Lefroy, headmistress 1898–1907, pointed out that her staff were laying the foundations which would lengthen the school life of

Rev. Professor Pearce, sub-warden of Durham University, and by other dons such as the Rev. F.B. Jevons, M.A. Oxon., tutor and examiner at the university.

The pupils responded admirably, achieving good results in the external examinations of Cambridge Local, Senior and Junior. Durham High School girls were providing indisputable evidence of the 'educability' of girls. The opening of degree courses to women, first in London in 1878, followed by Manchester in 1883 and Durham in 1895, gave the pupils further incentive – if any were needed.

Nevertheless, reservations about the benefits of the new academic opportunities for girls still surfaced occasionally. At the prize-giving ceremony in 1887, Canon Body raised concerns about the growing popularity of the 'cramming system' for

Above left: End of term registration report, signed by Elizabeth Gray, which includes attendance records and notes on subjects taught from 1891.

Left: A typical front cover from a register, 1888–9.

Above: 3 South Bailey, 1902. Note the girls studying through the open window on the ground floor.

Left: Miss Lefroy and the entire school, 1902.

girls. Some of the pupils could then take advantage of new career openings in teaching, thanks to a Teachers' Registration Bill going through Parliament.

Numbers in the school touched a hundred at the end of the century and there were nine old girls at universities and two more graduating with firsts in their B.Litt. degrees at Durham University. Miss E. Gertrude Griffiths, the first woman to inspect the school, wrote: 'The standard of work at this school is in some respects undoubtedly far in advance of that usually found in High Schools.'

As the new century got underway it became clear this was to be a challenging time of falling birth rates plus rising costs and educational standards. Nevertheless in the face of competition from a local authority secondary school for girls, the governing body signed a lease for new premises at Leazes House. Following Miss Headlam's three-year tenure, they also appointed an outstanding headmistress, Miss Stafford Smith, in 1911, and faced the first full inspection by the Board of Education the following year to establish the claim to be an 'efficient' educational institution.

Opposite: Miss Headlam, headmistress 1908–11.

Below: Daily exercise, or drill, was an important part of early school life.

From Hygiene Studies to History

From the beginning the school had endeavoured to give each girl as wide an education as possible. At the first Prize Day in 1885 it was stated that 'the High School had been formed to give a good education at a moderate price'. And as early as 1900 girls were exhorted to take up 'some definite work after leaving school instead of drifting into an aimless life of self indulgence'.

In 1912 Lady Londonderry, then Mayoress of Durham, said that she 'hoped the girls were learning to read and find out things for themselves, and were not content merely to have things poured into them'. She was very insistent that each girl should realize that her schooldays were only a beginning and that she should have some 'very definite plans for the work which she hoped to do on leaving school'.

In 1920 Miss Stafford Smith praised the parents 'because you have allowed to happen what I asked very specially for at the end of my first term here: you have sent your girls here earlier, so that they might enter on the school course at the beginning,

Below: The School, with Miss Headlam in the centre, towards the end of her tenure in 1911.

and you have left them here longer, so that they might have the full advantage of that course.'

But those who through illness or some other reason were unable to take this full course were not forgotten. In 1925 Miss Stafford Smith explained the founding of a 'Special Class' where girls would, instead of lessons in mathematics and languages, be given lessons in simple dressmaking, upholstery, hygiene, first aid, home nursing, simple account keeping and, possibly, typewriting. 'Such a course forms a sound foundation for girls who propose later on to be trained as hospital nurses, child nurses, housekeepers, missionaries, etc. – while it should fit girls to be intelligently useful in their own homes.'

In those earlier days, teachers did not specialize in single subjects, teaching all manner of disciplines from German and English to junior history and science. 'We had our first science lessons on the tables in the dining room with Bunsen burners attached to the gas jets and we experimented with water-filled tumblers in the cloakroom,' one girl recalled.

THE HIGH SCHOOL, DURHAM.

Classes will be formed in September for

DOMESTIC SCIENCE

Under Miss M. S. Dobson

(First Class Diploma for Housekeeping, Glasgow College of Domestic Science).

These classes will be open to girls over 17, who will be allowed to substitute them for those in certain subjects of the regular school curriculum, and, occasionally, on the recommendation of the Head Mistress, to certain younger girls for whom more than one foreign language may be found inadvisable.

Applications from outsiders will be considered, but the numbers in the classes will be strictly limited to secure individual attention.

Fees for Bye-Students, £3 3s. 0d. a term.

The scheme proposed for the year, September, 1913, to July, 1914, is :—

In the Autumn and Spring Terms—One class a week for Advanced Needlework, and one for Cookery.

In the Summer Term—One class a week for Advanced Needlework, and one for Housework.

Each class will probably be held from 2.15 to 3.45.

The Head Mistress will be glad to discuss the matter and to receive names before the end of July.

1913.

Left: Introduced in 1913, Domestic Science instantly became one of the more popular classes.

Bottom: A typical first form class room in Leazes, c.1920.

such a pleasant lesson, and one has no idea of the feeling one gets when one is first allowed to wash clothes, plunging elbows deep into lovely hot water, full of soap suds, and squeezing and pressing wet woollens … it is rather dull polishing furniture or glasses.'

In their 1913 report, the Board of Education's inspectors paid special tribute to that first governing body to whose public-spirited action the school owed its 'continuance'. The new headmistress, Miss Stafford Smith, already proving an asset, was 'admirable, being a stimulating and inspiring teacher, a clever organizer of school work and a safe custodian of the welfare of those entrusted to her care'. So committed was she that during a period of financial anxieties she admitted to paying two members of staff from her own pocket rather than lose them.

The domestic science class was popular: 'We have some jolly times, though of course we have to work as the marks go into the week's grades. The cookery lessons are the most interesting; and once or twice we have cooked for the school, but I don't think it was a success, at least the boarders didn't think so.'

Tuition in other household duties met with a mixed response, as this pupil reported: 'Laundry is

Last September, classes in Domestic Science, under Miss Dobson, were begun and have flourished. They are open to girls in the School over 17, who may substitute classes in Cookery, Dressmaking, &c., for one or two of the usual School Subjects. Outsiders also are welcomed.

The Things That Matter

The personality of Miss Stafford Smith – 'Staffy' – stands out as the driving force behind the school's success in the early twentieth century. One of her pupils described her as 'red haired and fiery tempered but an excellent teacher'. Her Christian principles were at the heart of her teaching. 'I trust no girls will leave this school without knowing what are the things that matter,' she said.

Miss Headlam wrote of her successor: 'Miss Stafford Smith found a little school in a narrow street; she handed to her successor a big school in a beautiful setting.'

'Staffy' was headmistress for 22 years, one year at the Bailey and twenty-one at Leazes House, so perhaps it is not surprising that memories of her abound: 'I remember her as a brisk person, always dressed in brown, of medium height, ageless, her red hair carefully braided, her grey-green eyes alert as she walked up the side of the hall to the dais, her prayer book and Bible tucked in the crook of her arm. She had a fascinating habit of wriggling her scalp when she was considering matters.

'We were all in awe of her, and indeed she could be very cross and was at times, but I don't think we were basically afraid of her. She taught throughout the school and enjoyed playing with the youngest children. She was an excellent teacher and although she didn't exactly suffer fools gladly she was rarely sarcastic and I remember some hilarious lessons with her'.

Opposite: Miss Stafford 'Staffy' Smith, 1915.

Left: A girl sits on the wall of Leazes House looking towards the city, c.1920.

A Prayerful Life

'Three things of importance were drummed into us,' one girl reported. 'First, the Christian and prayerful approach to life; second, manners towards each other and people in general (towards herself and the staff this was taken for granted); third, writing and spelling which produced basic literacy.'

Throughout her time at the school Staffy must constantly have faced financial difficulties. The move to Leazes House was followed closely by the First World War, then came the difficult years of the twenties and the recession of the early thirties. Despite all this the school achieved two boarding houses in Ravensworth Terrace and a fine playing field. The gardens were superbly well kept, by one

Above: Hockey first XI.

man and a boy, a delightful setting for the annual Garden Party – 'always on a fine sunny day!' However, the Jubilee Garden party in 1934, the year after Miss Stafford Smith left for family reasons, was remembered for the rain: '… unfortunately Saturday was very wet. The rain scarcely stopped until about 6 o'clock in the evening.'

Miss Stafford Smith had a hand in everything it seemed, from choosing the tennis team and ordering the menus, to how the girls sang *St Patrick's Breastplate* from the platform in the Town Hall on Speech Day.

'One of her less endearing habits was a daily or twice daily walk through the school during lessons,' a pupil recalled. 'One would suddenly become aware and so make others aware of a figure standing still outside the form room door. Backs straightened up, a more intelligent attention became apparent, probably thus warning the mistress in charge. It was rare but not unknown for the headmistress actually to interrupt a class, usually with dire consequences to some.'

The Importance of Fresh Air

Monica Hayton (née Dixon) was a pupil from 1920 to 1928 and her mother was one of the very first pupils at the school. Her daughter Jennifer also attended in the 1950s. Three generations of one family attending the same school! Monica remembers:

'We had to walk around the school after each lesson to have some exercise. Miss Stafford Smith was frightening, she had auburn hair and always seemed to wear clothes that were the same colour.

Durham High School. – Garden looking West.

Left: The rose arches, seen here looking west in 1933 with girls posing for the photograph in the background and (below left), looking east later on in 1940.

An Inspirational Place

Stability gradually improved with increasing numbers of weekly boarders, and the purchase of Leazes House in February 1925 was an important step towards a lasting future for the school. It was an inspirational place, as these recollections reveal:

'The main school building was an old house, with a very impressive front door, or so it seemed to us who were forbidden to enter. We had to make our way every morning to the back door and then hang coats and leave outdoor shoes in a very dark cloakroom.

'I remember the hot summer days when we had the windows open and could hear the crews on the river practising for the regatta and the birds singing and how hard it was to concentrate on work.

'School was a lovely old house with beautiful views across the school garden and the river to the cathedral and castle. The school garden and playing fields, sadly now the new road and multi-storey car park, were beautiful. An area known as the "logs" was popular with young girls. The trees were easy to swing on and climb. One in particular could have been purpose-built for youngsters. The "wall" which separated the upper and lower garden was paved, the "holy of holies" for the Upper Fifth and Sixth Formers. The lower garden had an area set as a stage, which was used for performances of Shakespeare's plays and vaulting displays in the summer.'

'… a super old house with lovely gardens which went down to the river. We always had a grandstand view of the regatta from the garden walls.'

At the back of the classrooms in Leazes House there was a small raised area, a platform, and we liked to sit at the desks there because you could see what was going on, but of course the teacher could see you more easily too.

'We used to walk along the river banks through Pelaw Woods to Old Durham Gardens where we had games lessons. We didn't have a science laboratory, we just had a cupboard and all the science equipment was kept in there. My favourite subject was needlework.'

Above: Leazes House, 1933.

'… those lovely old horse-chestnut trees were a marvellous source of some fine conker collections.'

'The school grounds were really beautiful – old rhododendrons and lovely flowering trees and pears to eat in the Autumn down near the netball court.'

'Our favourite part of the garden was an area called Leafy Hollow, which was very overgrown and natural, not part of the tended garden.'

'The garden was a wonderful place, full of hidden bits, tiny lawns where girls could sit and tell secrets and discuss the gossip of the school and have treasure hunts and scavenger hunts. It was the most marvellous place for games like hide-and-seek.'

However conditions were not perfect: 'When we first moved into Leazes House, the top classrooms, which had been bedrooms, still had their original wallpaper. I remember that our classroom was decorated with strings of large red roses.'

More Outside Toilets

'The day I went to the Big School I felt very grown up. We walked through the gates at the end of Leazes Place and down the drive to the big house – but, oh dear, more outside toilets.'

'We wore our scarves though we weren't supposed to and we fought over the front desks near the old gas fires.'

'Leazes House in the 1920s was quite a primitive sort of place. There were no labs, no art room, no domestic science block, no library even, just a cupboard in one of the form rooms. We had our own individual desks, of course, with ink wells set into them and refilled once a week and all lessons took place in the form room.'

'When I first went to school as a day girl we travelled by train. It was a long walk from the station over Framwellgate Bridge, through the

Opposite: A boarders bedroom, 1940.

Bottom right: Ella Wright in 1925 and 1928.

Market Place and up Claypath, and a long walk back up the station hill at the end of the day to catch the train. At that time too, the whole school was "aired" between lessons. The windows of the classrooms were flung wide open and each class walked downstairs, round the entrance hall and back again. The windows were closed and lessons proceeded.'

'Whenever we were a bit slow in answering questions Staffy would fling the window open even in the coldest weather, saying that we needed some fresh air. Sometimes it was very cold. We would sit on our hands to try to keep warm. Some of the form rooms had only a coke stove or an open fire, and one was either frozen or roasted depending on where one sat.'

A Red-Hot Poker
'There was no central heating or fireplace. Instead there was a large round iron stove in each room, heated by coke, around which was a fireguard. We had lots of fun putting pieces of rubber on top of the stove at the beginning of a lesson, which made a terrible smell. We were then in trouble!'

'Miss Stafford Smith had a – to us – annoying habit of always picking up the poker and poking the fire when she came into a room, whether it needed it or not. So one day we decided to teach her a lesson and we warmed the handle of the poker. She stopped her irritating habit!'

Ella Wright was a pupil from 1924 to 1934 and recalls discipline being 'strict but not severe'. She also has memories of the importance attached to

fresh air: 'You had to behave otherwise you were sent out and had to stand outside the door. Miss Stafford Smith walked round the school and if she found you outside the door you had to account for the reason. It wasn't a very pleasant encounter at all. In between every two lessons the whole school lined up and walked round the school in order to get some exercise and some fresh air. While we were out all the windows had to be opened. We had window monitors who opened all the windows for us and closed them when we went in. It wasn't considered good for children to sit for too long. Unless it was pouring with rain or snowing we all went out.'

The weekends too were a time for fresh air during the 1940s as former pupil Margaret Hardy remembers: 'On Saturdays we had to go out for a two-hour walk in the afternoon, juniors with a member of staff, seniors unescorted. On Sundays we only had to go out for one hour!'

TWO WORLD WARS

Two World Wars

'We were not sent home because of bombs or air raids. It seemed to affect us very little…'

In 1914 Miss Stafford Smith wrote:'It is a very strange task to edit the School Magazine this year. As one runs over the records of the events of 1914, it is scarcely believable that the events of the first two terms can possibly belong to the same year as those of the Autumn Term. All that happened before the outbreak of war seems cut off by a wide gulf from the strange present in which we find ourselves. We decided not to have the usual public Prize Giving … we felt that a public Prize Giving must necessarily be festive, and that festivities were out of place.'

The school felt that 'strange present' in little ways as these reports reveal:

'Miss Wilkinson left … intending to go to Paris in September: owing to the war she had to give up her plan.'

'In the last few weeks of the term [1915] we collected eggs every week and sent them to the

Above: Examples of the School Magazine, produced by pupils between 1919 and 1921.

Previous pages: Four generations of headmistresses gather with dignitaries at the 50th anniversary celebrations in 1934 (l–r): Miss Brown, Miss Stafford Smith, Mr Fowler (the Mayor), Mrs Owens (née Lefroy), Lady Gainford and Miss Headlam.

Above: The playing field and tennis courts, 1920s.

National Egg Collection for the Wounded. We also sent some parcels of old French books etc. for Belgians interned in Holland.'

In 1915 the general knowledge exam was entirely on the war, while in 1916 it was recorded that some girls '... went with Miss Feld to Newcastle to see Benson in *Hamlet*. The performance was good and fortunately there were no zeppelins about that night.'

On 21 November 1916 a War Savings Association was formed in the school and soon had 57 members (54 girls in school at the time) each depositing 'any amount from one penny upwards'.

The war had a big effect on numbers in the school, which had been steadily rising from the 11 original girls to 85 by the autumn of 1912. During the years of the war, scarcely more than 50 girls remained. Nevertheless it seemed that the educational aspirations of successive generations of girls were changing. Miss Stafford Smith recorded

the marked change in society's attitude to girls' education. The war, far from hindering progress, meant it was rapidly becoming a matter of course that girls should be trained for a profession, she said. By 1919 numbers had doubled and rose steadily again until the depression of the 1930s.

Women Take Their Place in the World

When Staffy announced her departure in 1933, Canon Dawson Walker, Chairman of the Governors, said: 'My dismay can be imagined. I was quite unprepared for this. I had come to accept Miss Stafford Smith as one of our well-established institutions. Her departure simply had not come within the horizon of my thoughts.'

Staffy's many achievements would be a lasting legacy. In 1934 Dr Hensley Henson, Bishop of Durham, rejoiced in the first 50 years of the school as a 'well-loved institution of Durham'. In those

Below: Pages from a leaflet advertising new uniforms, c.1940.

Right: Miss Brown.

No. 541.
BLAZER
(with Monogram).
S 7372 **22/6**
32 ins. Bust.
Rise or fall 6d. per inch.

KILTED SKIRT
(OPTIONAL)
Skirt is made on bodice.
Serge S 7373 **19/-**

Length 16 ins.
Rise or fall 6d. per inch.

No. 542.
TUNIC
Serge S7073 **22/6**
28 ins. from top of yoke.
Rise or fall 6d. per inch.
To be 2 inches above the knee
when kneeling.

No. 540.
OVERCOAT
(to open or close at neck).
Serge S 7581 **53/6**
32 ins. Bust, 36 ins. length.
Rise or fall 1/- per inch.

Kindly Note.—All the above Garments are Made to Measure.

years, 'the status, habit and outlook of the female sex have been revolutionized,' he said. 'All the doors of opportunity in the State now stand open to the girls as well as the boys; all knowledge has been brought equally to both. As citizens, lawyers, doctors and writers, women are taking their place in the world … A new sense of responsibility, a new consciousness of independence, a new power of self direction mark the young women of today.'

Miss Brown, headmistress from 1933–8, thought that 'good women, far more than good men, are the salvation of the world'. Miss Brown made a number of changes, as her successor Miss Jackson pointed out: 'It is difficult for those who have watched the gradual changes made during the time she was here to realize all that she did for the school. To her is due the introduction of a full-time mistress for physical education; the equipping of a laboratory for

chemistry; and many improvements in both the school and the boarding houses.'

One of the highlights of the 1930s was the opening of the music department in 1932. Shortly afterwards, botany and French were introduced while chemistry was still only provided 'for those who knew they would require it when they left school'. In 1934 Miss Brown made a 'definite attempt to widen the interests of the school, and put into the timetable a short period on Monday mornings for discussion of the events of the previous week'.

Quite a lot of girls left from the Upper Fifth after School Certificate but those going to Teacher Training College often spent one year in the Sixth Form. Medical students left at 17 to do 1st MB at medical school and those intending to go on to university stayed two or more years to take Higher Certificate. There were not, of course, statutory awards in those days and pupils from independent schools were not eligible for county grants, although they could enter for State Scholarships or university awards, of which there were very few for women. Both students and parents had to be dedicated to higher education.

Proper Science!

Science had a prominence from the earliest days of the school's history and endeavours were made to inspire the girls. In March 1922 for example, two distinguished gentlemen, Mr Armstrong and Mr Grey, gave a demonstration of wireless telegraphy and explained its elementary principle. By means of

a wireless set, which they brought with them, the girls heard music in Newcastle – but the school was situated too low for a very successful hearing!

Miss Brown made a significant contribution to the school's development by appointing a teacher to cover science 'properly'. Miss K.M. Jackson, a new graduate of Reading University, joined simultaneously with Miss Brown; she had not at that time seen the school – the two met and the appointment was made on the steps of the British Museum.

Science was playing an increasingly important role in the girls' curriculum thanks to Miss Jackson, whose approach gave scope to those girls whose bent was scientific rather than literary. And over the

Right: View from the Boarding House of the Cathedral, 1940s. Note the vegetable patches in the forground.

Above: Science lesson, 1949.

decades to come the significance of science was to become central to the school's mission – even though its beginnings were humble. Miss Jackson had been expecting less than perfect conditions but was not fully prepared for the laboratory consisting of a sink, two marble-topped wash-stands and a gas ring. Despite this, she stayed for six years though, overlapping with the headmistress of the same name. After starting with School Certificate botany and achieving encouraging results, Miss Jackson then introduced chemistry in a laboratory largely of

her own design which was also used as a form-room. The marble tops were the first things to go!

Two girls took a Higher School Certificate combining botany, chemistry and geography, all taught by Miss Jackson. One of these went to Newcastle University for a Science degree and was employed by ICI during the war years. Laboratory facilities were moved in the 1940s to an out-building: '… the old stables were converted into a laboratory, science prep room and art room. All girls were expected to attain their School Certificates and preferably "matric".

The latter matriculation was a basic necessity for entry to university and many academic trainings.'

The Headmistress's Report of 1935 noted that, of the five girls who had taken chemistry that term, three intended to study medicine. She longed for a time when they had a properly equipped laboratory and chemistry became a normal school subject. However, progress was being made in difficult circumstances, and she was glad to know that they could now prepare girls for one of the greatest professions, that of medicine.

Miss Jackson was headmistress for three years before moving on to Newcastle Church High School, but two years later, she was killed in a car accident: 'All who worked with her during those three difficult years of change from peace to war will long remember her bright personality, her great charm and manner and the unfailing help and encouragement which she gave. Lives like hers can ill be spared, and her loss is widely felt for her name was beginning to be known in the larger world of education where her originality of outlook and understanding of the problems involved would have been invaluable in the shaping of the school of the future.'

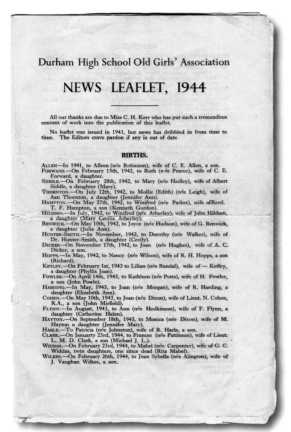

Left: Regardless of war, the news of births and deaths were still recorded in the back of the School Magazine, except in the case of 1944 where the editors make an apology at the top of the page!

The air raid siren was situated at the top of one of Durham Castle's turrets, as one girl remembered: 'We were not sent home because of bombs or air raids. It seemed to affect us very little. There was a large purpose-built air raid shelter in the garden near to the school. It was more fun as a recreational pleasure. It was partly above ground level at one end with a flat roof. We used to climb on to the top and jump off, starting at the shallow end and graduating to the deeper drop – most daring!'

It must have been difficult for parents to provide the girls with everything they needed but somehow they did. 'Clothes were rationed and a lot must have been handed down,' recalled another girl. 'Before the war the boarders used to have a Sunday dress of green serge with long sleeves but not many kept it up during the war, and there was no special wear

Gas Masks and Top Coats

During the Second World War the girls' participation was a little more active, as one pupil reported: 'Part of the school's war effort was for girls to go to a farming camp at Greta Bridge and help with the harvesting. This first took place in 1943 and we learnt to stook, stack and load barley, wheat and oats. Also we cooked and cleaned for us all on a rota system. It was my first experience of learning to drive a tractor in the fields. It must have been a very jerky and bumpy experience for those on the trailer.'

Another recalled: 'Those gas mask boxes and our top coats which must go with us everywhere, always! Little room for us in the classrooms.'

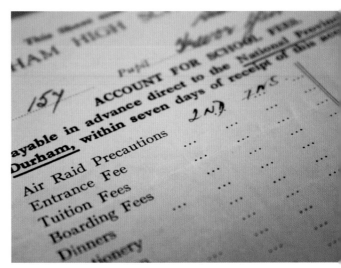

Above: School bill, including an entry for 'Air Raid Precautions', 1943.

Above: The Mayor, Cllr Cecil Ferens, at the launch ceremony of DHS and St Oswald's Church Sea Rangers boat, October 1948.

for games. I don't remember lessons often being interrupted by air raid warnings. These were more often during the night. We used to have to troop down to a cellar underneath one of the houses, where there were mattresses on the floor, and lie down there till the "all clear" went. We had to take a blanket, a torch and a game with us, and sometimes carry one of the little ones who were falling asleep by the time we came up again.'

Miss Sutherland, headmistress 1941–6, remembered that a large shrubbery was destroyed 'in order to grow vegetables: potatoes in the first year to clear the ground and then cabbages and then pigeons! How I hated them as they came to feast every evening!'

The school was fortunate, she added, to keep the cheerful cook throughout, but young women were called up and maids had to leave – 'I remember one morning trying to discuss St John's Gospel with the Lower Sixth while we peeled potatoes. After that we bought a peeling machine.'

Mutiny!

Another of Miss Sutherland's memories concerns the harvest camps: 'Will anyone forget the night I'd sent the girls who slept in the granary on to bed while I stopped at the farmhouse to 'phone and arrived to find a state of mutiny? They had seen a rat! I think it was the only time I was defied by Durham High School girls, but I had to give in and

Above: Miss Tanqueray with her pets.

Opposite: The only known photograph featuring the cellar shelter in Leazes House, 1959. The entrance can just be seen at ground level in the centre of the photograph.

we all trooped down through the rain to crowd into the cottage. To save face I had to return to the barn but I was scared and I've never prayed "Lighten our darkness" so sincerely before or since, even in an air raid.'

The cellars were strengthened and an air raid shelter was built for day girls but it was not considered safe to hold Speech Days in Leazes House. She added: 'Dean Alington, who was our Chairman, suggested that we use the Chapter House and I, for one, just loved Speech Days there, in spite of the difficult acoustics – Evensong in Durham Cathedral, that leisurely procession to the Chapter House, the Dean's witty remarks and the feeling of belonging to an ancient foundation.

'From the upstairs rooms one could see the cathedral and I remember well one night when every decoration on the tower was clearly visible in the moonlight and the drone of bombers was heard. It was soon after the "Baedeker raids" when other cathedral cities had been bombed so it might have been our turn … As I watched, up from the river rose a white mist and I thought how clever to use white smoke instead of the black they put up in industrial areas. It was, of course, river mist but it rose up round the cathedral and the bombers went away. A few weeks later the rumour spread that St Cuthbert had saved his Cathedral again – so legends are born.'

Margaret Rogers (née Hardy) was a pupil from 1939 to 1949 and recalls: 'An air raid shelter was build on one of the lawns and beyond this was an area where Miss Tanqueray kept ducks and some of

us kept rabbits or guinea pigs. In the garden before reaching the playing fields there was a market garden run by Miss Cleghorn. The laundry was done in the cellars of which two were where we had to go during night-time air raids with our sleeping bags, carefully avoiding the puddles after wash day.'

Grey Stew and Semolina

Actress Wendy Craig was also a pupil at the school during the war and recalls that the food was 'pretty terrible' in those days. 'Of course they must have struggled to feed us – and I recall a lot of grey-looking stew and semolina! We had to rush down to the basement when bombs were dropping but we

Below: The infamous 'hut', which began life as an army hut, and was brought to the school by Staffy in the 1920s where it remained until the erection of the new hall in 1951.

never thought about the war much as we were too busy getting on with our studies.'

Ms Craig boarded at school during the war because her parents were worried about travelling under threat of being bombed. 'When the warning siren went off all the boarders ran down to the basement and we huddled together in fear. The sound was terrifying and the building shook but thankfully stood firm.'

Wendy Craig was just five years old when she first went to DHS, little realizing that her acting debut there was to spark a lifelong career: 'I travelled by bus every day with my cousin Margaret. The school was always very warm and friendly and of course the cathedral was just across the river Wear, looming big and beautiful. It held an atmosphere of

welcoming safety. We were within the sound of cathedral bells and on special occasions we would celebrate in the glorious building. We would make our way through Durham town centre and over the bridge to the cathedral in a long green crocodile. I was a dreamy child and used to imagine that I was a pilgrim on my way to worship.

'We would often enjoy walks through secluded paths lined with rhododendrons by the river, we played in old trees in a secret grove and had so many imaginary games. There were even ducks in a muddy patch of the garden and we would go down to collect their eggs … I was very happy.'

Every morning she remembered the whole school gathering for prayers and a short service which was taken very seriously. 'I remember one

Above: The School in Diamond Jubilee year, 1944, featuring a young Wendy Craig (below in detail).

morning being sent out of assembly during a fit of the giggles. I still remember how appalled I felt standing outside the door, red-faced with shame. I suppose the desire to say prayers on a regular basis came from the teaching I received at school and it was a discipline which has stayed with me. Our hymn book was called *Songs of Praise* and because we had good music teachers who were passionate about what they played, the accompaniment was always superb. The voices and the instruments fired up in me a great enthusiasm to the point when, one day during choir practice, the teacher said: "Wendy Craig, please stop singing so loudly. You are spoiling it for the others!"'

An Acting Debut

Ms Craig's first teacher was Miss Morgan: 'She had plump, rosy cheeks and black curls and she used to read aloud to us while we sat cross-legged on the floor around her, trying to get as close to her as possible.'

The school hall in those days was a long wooden hut adjacent to the main house. It was also the gymnasium, theatre and chapel and it was here that she performed her first play in front of an audience – *The Little Red Hen*.

THE POSTWAR YEARS

CHAPTER 3

The Postwar Years

'... buildings, however grand, do not create a school. That depends on the personalities within it, and in full measure Durham High School was blessed.'

In her farewell to the school Miss Sutherland said: 'I am feeling very conscious of the way in which I have grown into Durham High School during my five years as headmistress and how much I am going to miss it all; not only miss you all but the cherry trees on the lower lawn, the view from my study window, dropping down through the garden and on to the river bank early in the morning on my way to the cathedral, Houghall Woods in bluebell time, the satisfaction of thinking that the linoleum in the hall is wearing well, that Mrs Binks was indeed a good friend when she helped me plan the kitchen and how well the green edges to the windows in the hut look. But most of all I shall miss people.'

Miss Todd came to the school in 1946 during the period of postwar difficulties, and reportedly 'she gave untiring energy to the programme of expansion

Previous pages: Charmian Welsh, with Miss Salter at the opening of the Sports Hall in 1975.　　　　　*Above: A class in 1949.*

Right: Miss Todd.

Below: The full contingency of staff, c.1950.

and development … the completion of the much-needed studio and laboratory building begun under Miss Sutherland, and the realization of the 20-year-old dream of a new school hall. Miss Todd exercised vigilance over beams, contractors and workmen on the site. How much the school owes to her in this connection as well as in all the aspects of normal school life, only those who were privileged to be on her staff can now realize.'

Although the Jubilee Building Fund was started in 1934 it was to be more than 15 years later, in 1950, that a 'proper' hall was constructed. In 1949 Miss Todd wrote:

Above: The new additions to Leazes House, c.1955.

'Our great hope is that we may soon be able to give more precise information about the new hall … the top of a hill is not the easiest place on which to expand, problems are made to be overcome, and it is conceivable that the fun of the battle for victory over them may even equal the future thrill of achievement.

'It was on 17 May 1950 that the little orange workmen's hut made its appearance, and throughout the succeeding months the school worked to the accompaniment of hammer and cement mixer and had the interesting experience of watching the long-awaited new hall take shape. It was sufficiently ready, but only just, for the school to assemble in it for the September term, and we shivered in it through a particularly cold and damp half-term until the full heating supply was laid on, pretending that we liked a temperature of 45 degrees.'

Miss Todd recalls that one Junior girl, on seeing the orange workmen's hut, said rather doubtfully that she didn't think the new hall would be big enough!

A Splendidly Modern Building

When Jenifer Blair joined Lower Second in September 1949 at the age of seven, the first big excitement was, she says, the completion of the new hall.

'It seemed such a splendidly modern building in comparison with the wooden hut which it replaced,' said Miss Blair, now Secretary of the Old Girls' Association. 'We suddenly had a large hall for playing in during break and lunch hour when it was raining – though I doubt that was the main consideration when the building was planned! I remember one rowdy game of "tag" when one girl fell and crashed into the hardboard which formed the front of the stage. She was less damaged than the stage, which was never the same again. The apron had to remain in place permanently to hide the dent in the front of the stage proper. The stage was, however, a great asset for school plays and the occasional dancing display.'

Our Own Peg and Shoe Locker

The completion of the hall meant that the hut became 'the dining hut' and the room previously used as the dining room became the main cloakroom. 'We all had our own peg and shoe locker – woe betide anyone who left their indoor shoes overnight in the locker instead of putting them in the shoe bag, which hung on her peg. Anything left lying in the cloakroom was put in the Fines' Cupboard presided over by the prefects. A small sum (one or two pennies) had to be paid in order to reclaim one's possessions.'

There was also a one-way system for leaving and entering the cloakroom – round the back passage for the way out and through the door in the main entrance hall for the way in. 'All of us at one time or another tried to sneak out through the "in" door as it was much more convenient,' Miss Blair recalls. 'Most attempts were foiled by the prefect on duty but occasionally we got away with it.'

Opposite: The sack race, sports day on the playing fields, 1950.

Inset: Jenifer Blair in 1949.

Games lessons meant a swift walk down a steep path to the netball and tennis courts and Miss Blair remembers that there were many moans and groans as the girls made their way back up the hill at the end of the lesson. 'There was a piece of land within the grounds earmarked for a hockey pitch. It had previously been cultivated as a market garden and it was a very stony piece of ground. Any form reported to the head for misbehaviour would be condemned to picking up stones during break and lunch hour for a longer or shorter period.'

Hockey entered the curriculum late in Miss Blair's school career, she says, 'but I remember that when the weather made it impossible to play outside, we were taken into the hall and had to practise with a sock over the hockey stick to protect the floor and to use a pompom-style ball to prevent broken windows.'

When Miss Todd left, while Miss Blair was still in Junior House, Miss Fenton took over. 'Every week she would appear when we were being taught by our form mistress and would go through the mark book. Those of us with uneasy consciences dreaded these occasions. If homework had not been handed in the letters "ngi" (not given in) would appear in the mark book and Miss Fenton would demand an explanation – which she rarely found acceptable. The reason for poor marks was also sought and advice for improvement given. Similarly,

at the end of each term we each had an interview with Miss Fenton and our form mistress to discuss our reports.'

There was an assembly each day, simply referred to as 'prayers'. When the bell for prayers went, everyone had to stop talking at once, line up at the form room door and then march, form by form, in silence, to the hall. When everyone was assembled it was the head girl's duty to inform the headmistress and to accompany her into the hall.

All bells were rung manually. A large hand bell was kept in the entrance hall and ringing it was one of the duties performed by the prefects. There was usually a prefect on duty in the library during a study period and this prefect would ring the bell at the end of the lesson.

Banana and Raspberry Jam Sandwiches

Miss Blair says prefects were also accorded the privilege of a Prefects' Tea, usually known as 'Prees Teas'. 'These were held on a Friday after school and two prefects were allowed into the town at lunchtime to buy cakes from Earl's, which was the best confectioner's in the city, until Miss Connie Earl retired. (I think this would be in the 1960s.) It was at a 'Prees' Tea' where I became addicted to banana and raspberry jam sandwiches!'

Prefects were frequently asked to sit with a class. 'When a teacher was absent on one occasion when my mother – who taught dancing – was ill, I was asked to teach her classes all afternoon,' Miss Blair

High School Knickers

The school was an exceptionally happy place in which to grow up, Miss Blair says, although the school rules were stricter in those days. For example: 'You were not allowed to eat so much as a sucked sweet if you were outside the school grounds and wearing school uniform. And we weren't allowed to go out of school without having our school hats on. We had to have indoor and outdoor shoes. The knickers had to be bottle green

recalls. 'I was only in the Upper Fifth (Year 11) but the classes were all in Junior House. A member of Junior House staff sat at the back to ensure all went smoothly, but that actually made it more nerve-racking for me. My mother's pianist had been cancelled, so another member of my form took her place. Unfortunately we had to exist on music from the song cupboard and it was quite amazing how many exercises I could teach, using *Sweet Lass of Richmond Hill* and *O for the Wings of a Dove*.

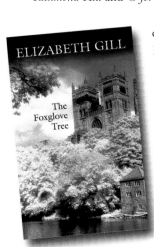

'Ballet has always been one of my interests and I loved the books written by Lorna Hill and was very proud that she was an Old Girl. Her books are still collected today – I recently saw one of them offered for sale at a price of £300. Another Old Girl who has more recently succeeded as a novelist is Elizabeth Gill.'

in winter and yellow-and-white checked gingham in summer to match our summer dresses – one of the reasons was that the grass sloped down towards the river and we were made to keep to the paths until a certain point in the summer term when an announcement was made that we were allowed to go on the grass. And that, apparently, was partly why we had to have yellow-and-white checked knickers, so that when we turned handstands we would look nice.'

School plays in those days were performed with a minimum amount of money so costumes had to be made of all sorts of weird and wonderful things. 'If you look at some of the pictures of the plays that we did in the past, you'll see that those famous High School knickers came into things. People wore a tunic over the top and they became a Roman soldier, or guards for the Dragon King; that was in a play called *Where the Rainbow Ends* in about 1959 I think, because I remember being in it. I was the Dragon King!'

Above: The 1961 production of Noah.

Left: Jenifer Blair, seen here second from right as the 'Dragon King' in the 1959 production of Where the Rainbow Ends.

Above: Guides and Brownies, 1949.

Gentle Care

Kathlyn Standring (née Joyce) became a pupil in September 1947, just after her eighth birthday. 'I joined ten other members of the Lower Second form, housed that year at 12, Leazes Place. I settled in immediately and thrived under the gentle care of my new form teacher, Miss Cartmell, who was the very antithesis of the screaming harridans who had taught me in my previous school. Her teaching was stimulating and, to this day, I can still see Miss Cartmell, surrounded by her small charges, pointing out and describing the Georgian doorways of Durham.

'The following September we became the Upper Second, with Miss Gill as our form mistress, and moved to the main school in Leazes House. Lessons became rather more formal, with new subjects including oral French appearing on the curriculum. It was at this point that I joined the school Brownie Pack, whose Brown Owl was Miss Tanqueray, the school matron. I remember being enrolled, learning new skills, playing games and singing songs but I cannot remember whether I was an elf, a sprite, a pixie or a fairy.

'I moved from form to form and "flew up" from the Brownies to the school's Guide Company. Life in those postwar years was austere, though I don't think I realized it at the time. Central heating was an undreamed-of luxury and we had to make do with a coal fire in each classroom. If your desk was close to the fire you roasted, while everyone else in the room shivered, but such was life in the 1940s and early 50s.

'Food was monotonous and unappetizing, even to an unfussy eater like me and the memory of trying to swallow congealed lumps of sago or tapioca pudding still makes me feel nauseous. It was bad enough for day girls but how much worse must it have been for the boarders who had no home-cooked meals to look forward to in the evenings and at weekends? No wonder then that at break time the younger boarders stared longingly at the tempting snacks that some of us brought from home, since all that was provided for them was a plate of bread and margarine.'

Above: Girls continue the tradition of sitting on Leazes 'wall', c.1955.

A Very Painful Experience

Another former pupil, Jane Young (née Powell) started school in 1952 at the same time as Miss Fenton. 'I remember meeting the previous headmistress (Miss Todd) with my parents and being given my hat badge and tie,' she recalls. 'Jumpers and cardigans came from the Scotch Wool Shop in Durham and the rest of the uniform came from Isaac Waltons in Newcastle.

'We lived in Gilesgate so I walked to school on my first day with my mother. I took my teddy and was absolutely terrified. In fact I screamed! I hadn't been to a nursery school or playgroup, the usual pattern today and found school a very painful experience. Our teacher, Miss Davison, was very

pleasant. We all had an animal on our cloakroom peg and work books. Mine was a red kangaroo. I remember playing in the wendy house and sandpit. We had a percussion band and everyone wanted to play the triangle. During prayers a teacher called Mrs Moore used to walk around to see if we all had our eyes closed! The present Queen's coronation took place while I was in Kindergarten and I still have the scrap book I made in school for the occasion.'

The school inspired Ms Young to become an ecologist: 'My very first nature study lesson was in the Autumn term 1955 with Miss Harrison, a teacher for whom I had the greatest admiration. She taught us about a kitten. In the middle of the lesson

Inset: Jane Powell in her new Junior House uniform, 1952.

*Below: From l–r: Margaret Stanley, Caroline Wood, Jane Powell,
Kathryn Powell, Jane Minto and Eileen Wood, 1955.*

the door opened and a grey cat walked in. It seemed like magic to me, a seven year old! From then on I always wanted to study biology.

'We walked through the gates at the end of Leazes Place and down the drive to the big house – but oh dear, more outside toilets! The school grounds were very large and had lovely gardens right down to the river banks. There were several sweeping lawns, trees and shrubs, netball and tennis courts and a hockey pitch. It was the most marvellous place for games like hide-and-seek. We had crazes for several games – hopscotch, hula hoop, countries, skipping and two ball (both with sung or said rhymes). Our Upper Second form teacher, Mrs Mulkerrin, used to come in every morning to find us all in groups on the floor playing jacks or chucks!'

No Squeaking Allowed

When Miss Salter became headmistress there was a tightening up of discipline and uniform, according to Ms Young. 'We all had to wear exactly the same, although there was a choice of two styles of indoor shoes and two styles of outdoor shoes. Hair had to be short or tied back. West of England tweed suits were introduced for the sixth formers. We were measured for these at Isaac Waltons in Newcastle and the skirt had to reach the floor in a kneeling position.

'Speech Days were always well rehearsed and I recall having to stand up and sit down numerous times on those squeaky green chairs without making them squeak! Through the discipline and expected high standard of behaviour, I think most girls felt that they were part of a school that was worth belonging to.'

Above: The idyll of sports day in the mid-1950s, not long before the controversial road scheme began in earnest.

End of an Era

In 1961 the school magazine announced: 'July 1961 brings us to the end of an era in the history of Durham High School. With great regret, for economic and staffing reasons, the boarding house is closing.'

But High School headmistresses are quick to seize opportunities, and the sadness of the passing of an era became pleasure in the appearance of 'new' rooms for art, music and needlework in the old boarding houses.

It might have been hoped that with plenty of space, both inside and out, the school could continue on its steady progress. However, progress of a different kind overtook those hopes as the new Durham City 'through road' was planned to march right through the school gardens. The tale of these difficult years – and their happy outcome – is best told by Miss Salter, who, as headmistress from 1958 to 1978, took the school through this major crisis in its history.

'When I was being interviewed for the post of headmistress of the High School in January 1958, I was warned by the Chairman, Dean Wild, that a Through Road Scheme might affect the school playing field, but that the Governors had met the Planning Authority with a view to resolving the difficulty. He also told me that the lease of Junior House, at the end of Leazes Place, was coming to a close, and I was asked if I thought the Junior School should continue in another place. I remember being very emphatic in my reply that the Junior School was an essential part of the whole.

Above: A road scheme meeting in the Town Hall, c.1960. Seated on Miss Salter's left is the architect, Matthew Hayton.

Box and Cox

'By September 1958, the Junior School had closed in Leazes Place, and was surviving in temporary accommodation in the boarding house in Ravensworth Terrace. I need not dwell on the problems of Box and Cox for the boarders and juniors. Suffice it to say that the architect, Mr Matthew Hayton, had undertaken to provide a beautiful set of classrooms, purpose-built for juniors, by January 1959 – and this he did. How fortune blessed us in having Mr Hayton as Governor, parent, architect and friend, the succeeding years were to prove.

'It is amusing now to rifle through the files of cuttings from *The Durham Advertiser* and to see such headings as "Crisis Passed". Little did we know what was in store for us. One cutting, on the day

Dean Wild opened the new Junior House, shows him sitting with a group of Kindergarten boys and girls, who seem to be showing him their books – the heading is "The Dean's turn to listen."' Without Dean Wild's tact and patience, the history of the school might have been very different, if indeed there had been a school at all.

Opposite, below: Ravensworth Terrace boarding houses before the road scheme demolition.

Below: Story time in the new Junior House with Dean Wild.

Right: Girls from Junior House, accompanied by Miss Salter, help with the tree planting ceremony, 1967.

Below: Bulldozers move in on the old playing fields, 1966.

'Three years later the decision was made to close the boarding house. This was a heart-rending decision, taken after much thought and discussion. There were 30 boarders and 300 day girls by this time. Problems of staffing at weekends grew greater, and the day school was making demands on the space, as numbers grew. In the report by Her Majesty's Inspectors in 1961 we were advised to expand even more, and so we were able to develop a very fine studio and a music room in the old dormitories.

'Another interesting reference may be made to the cost of these adaptations; for the total sum of £400, given by the Sir John Priestman Charity, an ordinary classroom was transformed into a well-equipped geography room – this included the cost of tables, stools, map cupboards, blackboards, blackout and screen. The projector was given by the Parents' Association'.

Doom and Gloom

'It was very soon after these alterations that the clouds began to reappear on the horizon about the Through Road Scheme. One Friday morning in March 1962 we read in *The Durham Advertiser* that the Ministry of Transport had agreed to the scheme. There was a sketch map of the centre of the city, marking in heavy black type two roundabouts and the proposed road, including our buildings and taking up the whole of our playing space. Headlines appeared week after week expressing doom and gloom for Durham High School's prospects.

'Governors, staff, parents and Old Girls were all involved in discussions. When it was announced that the High School may have to move, speculation

Above: Cover and inside page from a booklet advertising the new School, 1967.

about alternative sites began and some clashes with other people's interests occurred. A Public Inquiry was set up in January 1963, at which the Dean, Mr Hayton and I were present. It became clear that our plans to stay on at the Leazes House site were to be frustrated. After four days of meetings in the unheated Town Hall, I well remember hurrying home to Leazes Place on the Friday evening to prepare to go to the Parents' Association dance. I was late, tired, depressed – and not ready when my escort arrived. I remember calling from the bathroom to my mother, "Give him a drink!" It was Professor Fisher, one day to be Chairman of the Governors. As we set off, we decided that we must look cheerful when we met the parents.'

A Lasting Bond

'The following five years were a continual nightmare of meetings, appeals, more gloomy headlines, more changes of plan, until in March 1967 the Dean was at last able to state that plans had been passed, compensation agreed and the appeal for further funds had been successful. A tree-planting ceremony took place with the whole school assembled at Farewell Hall. It was windy and raining, the microphones did not work but we were happy. Those difficult days had created a bond between the Governors and parents which remains to this day.

'Meanwhile the Through Road Scheme had been going ahead since 1964, and the school building

Previous pages: Marjory Soar (née Robertshaw), who was head girl in 1966, had the honour of planting a tree to inaugurate the new building.

Below: Miss Salter looks on (left) as pupils begin their first day at Farewell Hall, January 1968.

stood on a promontory with the road works continuing around us. Buses took the girls to games in various parts of the city and the disturbance was considerable. Mrs Tait was congratulated on keeping the physical activities going during the three years of waiting for the new school, but what joy when, once again, Mr Hayton was able to promise that we could

move into the new buildings in January 1968 – and, as before, his promise was kept.'

Former pupil Monica Hayton recalls the move to Farewell Hall: 'This was a very difficult time, and it went on for ages. Losing the grounds meant there wasn't any room to expand. Matthew [Mrs Hayton's husband, architect of the new school] and

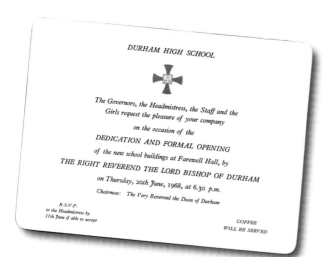

Left: Invitation to the official opening of Farewell Hall, June 1968.

Below: The library shortly after opening.

When the Bishop of Durham dedicated the new school in June 1968, he chose as his theme the name of the site in its original meaning. FARE WELL was a good omen for the future. 'My brief for this contribution was the removal to Farewell Hall, but I should not like to close without saying that buildings, however grand, do not create a school. That depends on the personalities within it, and in full measure Durham High School was blessed.'

Marjory Soar (née Robertshaw) was head girl in 1966: 'I had the great honour of planting a tree to inaugurate the new building at Farewell Hall,' she says. 'The event was televised by Tyne Tees Television which was then in its infancy. At the event, Mr Matt

Miss Salter went to lots of meetings. Without Miss Salter the school could have foundered. She was very determined. The problem was that only the garden was compulsorily purchased, which made it very hard to find another site. They looked at several; one on Potters Bank by St Mary's College and another near the obelisk in North End. Thankfully, in the end Durham University offered the school the Farewell Hall site. They were only allowed to build a replacement school to the same dimensions as Leazes House so Matthew measured everything, every cupboard, every alcove. This was why the new school was too small almost as soon as it was built.'

Farewell Hall

Mr Daynes, the caretaker, remembering his old army days, organized a system of packing and labelling which proved almost foolproof, and on a dark morning in January 1968, everyone arrived at Farewell Hall.

The first morning was spent in arranging for the children to be shown round the entire building before settling into their own classrooms. The building seemed very large after Leazes House, but it was not long before funds for extensions were being sought.

Left: Needlework, 1978.

Below: The new sports hall under construction, 1975.

Hayton, the architect, presented me with a beautiful trowel which is one of my treasured possessions.' That bit of school history continues, since in November 2008 pupil Emily Morris became the millionth person to plant a tree nationally for the Woodland Trust's 'Tree for All' campaign.

For some, the 'new school' took a bit of getting used to: 'How we disliked the new building; no feeling, no atmosphere, no long dark servants' passages'. Leazes House had been 'school' to Durham High School girls for more than 50 years and provided many memories for both staff and pupils. It had been 'like a large, family home'.

More Room

In 1973 a two-form entry to Senior School was established, not only increasing the number of subjects taught, but necessitating more rooms in which to teach them. In 1970 an extension to the

Opposite: Miss Salter attending the Buckingham Palace Garden Party, June 1969.

Left: Miss Salter, Charmian Welsh, and Dean Heaton at the opening of the Sports Hall, 1975.

dining room was completed and, in 1975, the sports hall was officially opened:

'The long-awaited opening of the Sports Hall took place on Saturday 18 October. Miss Charmian Welsh [Olympic diver] graciously accepted our invitation to return to her old school in order to perform the opening ceremony … the actual ceremony took place outside, in the school courtyard. Everyone assembled enthusiastically around one of the entrances to the hall. Despite the cold, Miss Welsh, armed with a large pair of scissors, officially pronounced the building open, and snipped the ribbon. To everyone's surprise, there was already an enthusiastic game of tennis in progress.'

Right: A spread from the appeal brochure, 1977.

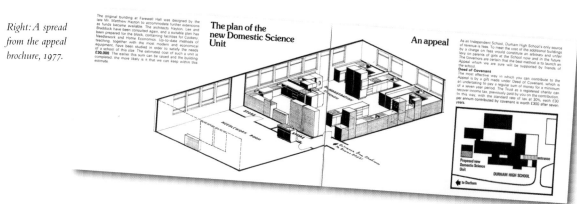

Left: Dean Heaton, Miss Salter and Monica Hayton, Matthew's wife, at the opening of the Salter Wing in 1977.

Below: Miss Salter at her retirement party in 1978.

In 1977 a new domestic science block was opened and named the Salter Wing. A year later, Miss Salter retired. Dean Wild, himself already retired, wrote of her that she had 'devoted herself to the school entirely and enthusiastically, right through to the end of her teaching career…'

It should not be forgotten that the negotiations with the Local Authority regarding the Through Road Scheme extended over no less than seven years, and throughout this long period the prospects for the school remained hazardous. In this daunting situation Miss Salter's confidence and courage never faltered. The prolonged search for a new site for the school ended successfully at Farewell Hall. Then there was the problem of raising funds. Here again Miss Salter was indefatigable. It seldom falls to any headmistress to transfer a school to an entirely new site, and then to stay long enough to see it firmly established in its new home and even more flourishing than before. This was Miss Salter's achievement.

Hamish and Andrew

Former sports captain Katherine Anderson (née Gill) has fond memories of Miss Salter: 'She had dogs and she used to walk around the school with her dogs and we used to enjoy looking at them and stroking them when she was walking past – that was what she expected us to do. She was very friendly, but we were also a bit nervous about Miss Salter.'

Miss Salter's dogs, Hamish and Andrew, were famous. They appear in many school photographs, unofficial and official. One ex-member of staff, Carol Smale, remembers going to see Miss Salter in her office. Andrew was fussing round Carol when Miss Salter told him, 'Sit down, Andrew, and leave Auntie Smale alone!'

The dogs' dinner always arrived on a tray from the kitchen at 12 noon and was consumed on the rug in front of the fire in the headmistress's office.

Kathryn Waters (née Powell), a pupil at the school from 1954–66, recalls Miss Salter bringing

Below: Andrew, Miss Salter's West Highland Terrier, seen here on the right with one of the caretaker's dogs. He could be found in many school photographs, as could his predecessor, Hamish.

Hamish into school each day. 'Hamish was a West Highland Terrier and he spent most of his free time in the Headmistress's study, but, occasionally, we were asked, during free periods, if we could take the dog for a short walk. One year, in 1965, Hamish starred in a short play called *We Are Not Amused*, written by Laurence Housman which was produced as part of the annual Speech Day and Distribution of Prizes.'

18th February 1983

A Cube

Sides 10cm

10cm

10cm

10cm

We have found

1l of water wei...

1L has the volu...

...le know ... 1l

CHAPTER 4

The 1980s

'... among the challenges of the future would be a fundamental change in education, interrelated with a technological revolution which was to affect all aspects of school life.'

A Centenary Celebration

The planning for the school centenary in 1984 had started two years before with the formation of a centenary committee, the designing of the centenary logo and the beginnings of a search

Above: Miss Stephenson plants a tree during the 1984 celebrations.

Previous pages: Junior House pupils enjoy a science lesson, 1983.

for addresses so that every possible Old Girl and past member of staff could be contacted.

Soon the Old Girls 'Link' project got under way, enabling present pupils to correspond with Old Girls of different generations. Meanwhile a group of parents had begun work on a recently acquired piece of waste land designated for a nature reserve. This was part of a grander scheme for the coordinated planting of trees, native woodland and more exotic specimens, in different areas of the grounds; and each of the headmistresses present at the centenary celebrations planted one.

The school office turned into (among other things) an archives room and was the headquarters of centenary planning. Then on 4 December 1983 Professor Fisher, Chairman of the Governors, unveiled a plaque in Bishop Cosin's Library to commemorate the meeting held there on 4 December 1883 – at which the decision was taken to open a school for girls.

It was decided that the period of celebration should run from March to September, beginning with Junior Speech Day and ending with Senior Speech Day, with the whole school joining

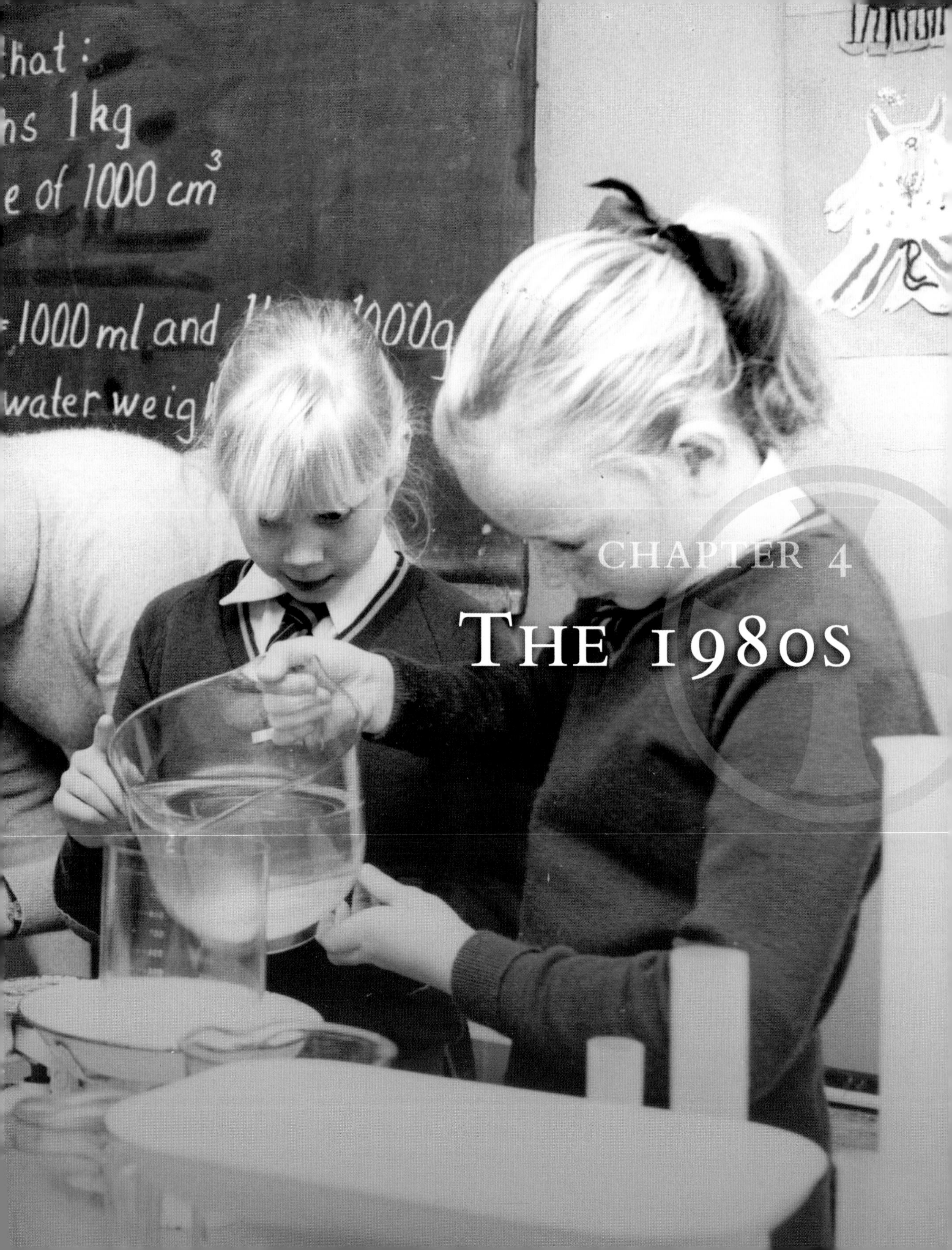

CHAPTER 4

THE 1980S

Durham High School Junior House
presents
JERUSALEM JOY
by Roger Jones
in the School Hall
Monday March 5th 1984
ADULT   7.00 p.m.
£1

Left: Poster and ticket from Junior House's 1984 production of Jerusalem Boy.

Below: From l–r: Miss Todd, Miss Stephenson, Miss Sutherland, Miss Salter and Miss Fenton at the centenary celebrations.

together for the focal point of it all – the Centenary Weekend, 5–7 May.

Junior House presented *Jerusalem Joy*, a cantata for children by Roger Jones which tells the whole Easter story, from the entry into Jerusalem to the Resurrection appearances. Then on four successive weekends the juniors took it to local churches. Later in March the pianist Janusz Stechley gave a Centenary Concert in Dunelm House with a programme entirely of Chopin.

Birthday Candles

The actual date of the school's birthday fell on Sunday 29 April. On the Friday there were festivities in school – a birthday cake, with candles (only ten, for safety's sake), and the presentation by the Governors of a centenary mug to each pupil.

On Friday 4 May all of the five Headmistresses covering the years from 1941 to 1984 met with the

Governors in school and, on the following day, they joined the Governors, staff past and present, Old Girls and families, parents, pupils and friends of the school to fill the cathedral. The Service was one of thanksgiving for 100 years of Durham High School and an act of re-dedication was led by Bishop Michael Ramsey, whose own association with the school was of long standing.

A Victorian Tea Party

That afternoon Farewell Hall was transformed back to the 1880s, and in its new guise 'opened' by Miss H.M. Harrison, President of the Old Girls' Association. A Victorian classroom replaced the familiar one, Victorian needlework and a Victorian tea-party were on offer and even the present-day tea was served by Victorian waitresses.

Outside, Junior children danced round a maypole and everywhere happy people were greeting each other under a bright sun – which prompted comparisons from those who, at the Jubilee celebrations 50 years previously, had spent most of the afternoon rescuing their displays from the downpour which marred the occasion.

Woggarts

The opera *The Woggarts of Weardale* was commissioned for the centenary, with music by Richard Addison and a libretto by Sybil Marshall. It tells a folk story of how little folk jealously guard

Right: Programme, ticket and the cast of the opera, The Woggarts of Weardale, *specially commissioned for the celebrations.*

Opposite: Dancing around the maypole as part of the festivities.

their very own primroses and punish anyone who dares touch them – and how the spell can be broken only by loving persistence. It was an ambitious project but after some anxious times in rehearsal it came together and was an experience long to be remembered by all involved in it.

While the school settled down to work again the Parents' Association was still busy, organizing a fashion show and planning the Centenary Dinner Dance to be held in September. A beautiful cup was presented to the school and, after examinations were over, the girls were back on the scene and the whole school took part in a sponsored walk. The substantial sum of money raised, along with that from the collection at the cathedral service, went to St Catherine's Anglican High School in Lesotho, with which the school established a centenary link which has gone from strength to strength (see Chapter 5).

Madam

Senior Speech Day in September, held for the first time in the sports hall and attended by some 900 people, was made very special by the presence of a most distinguished Guest of Honour, Dame Ninette de Valois, founder of the Royal Ballet School.

Much has already been written about the power of her presence in the Royal Ballet School, where she

was always addressed simply as 'Madam'. Out of respect to her (and also out of consideration for her arthritis) it was arranged for her to sit to present the prizes and instead of shaking hands, as was usual, each recipient curtseyed to her before receiving her award.

Headmistress Barbara Stephenson had been invited to meet Dame Ninette and she recalled a rather anxious moment: 'After taking tea together, less than an hour before the start of the evening's event, Dame Ninette suddenly asked: "What would you like me to talk about?" I was told afterwards that my face registered a moment of anxiety! I think I said that any of her experiences would be of interest, linked with any advice or encouragement she felt able to give the girls. I need not have worried: the audience sat spellbound as she recounted, among other things, what it had been like to be stranded in Paris, where I think she must have been performing, at the outbreak of the Second World War. When she was clearly

Ninette de Valois rehearses at Sadlers Wells, London, 1931.

approaching the point of drawing her address to a close, and perhaps wondering how best to do that, it was done for her as everyone spontaneously burst into loud and prolonged applause.'

Computers on the Curriculum
'As I have looked over the reports from the centenary year to my retirement in 1992, the memories of all this have come back,' Miss Stephenson added. 'It became obvious during the 1980s that among the challenges of the future would be a fundamental change in education, interrelated with a technological revolution which was to affect all aspects of school life.'

Already in 1983 a new building, to be named the Fisher Building, had been provided, housing an art studio and computer room. A new subject, computer studies, appeared on the curriculum, and within a very short time the cross-curricular application of the new technology began to have an impact.

Susan Egglestone was the first computer studies teacher. She was appointed in March 1983. 'I set up the first Tandy DOS network in the tiny room 26 situated in the newly finished Fisher Building, overlooking the site of the Nature Reserve. The room housed a main computer which had to be booted up manually every morning by moving switches to load up the 5¼-inch disc while the girls' machines used audio cassettes for storage. The girls from examination classes even chose names for their favourite computer.'

Many changes of venue, operating system and network technology have taken place over the years.

Left: Mrs Egglestone oversees pupils working on the brand new BBC Micro machines.

Above: Aerial view of the School, 1989.

If you happen to wander into the ICT suite today you are likely to find pupils engaged in movie production and editing, modelling clay animation and web design along with the more traditional uses of computers for word processing skills.

A Cosy Fireside Chat

Val Dunsford was a member of staff from 1986 to 2003 – first as a modern languages teacher, then as Head of Languages, then Head of Sixth Form and finally as Deputy Head. She was interviewed by Miss Stephenson back in 1985 and says: 'Her style was not to interview formally but to hold a cosy fireside chat. She probably found out more about me in the relaxed atmosphere of that cosy chat than any formal interview could have told her. I was late arriving for my interview as I wasn't sure whether the building in the dip on South Road was a school or not. At the time it wasn't felt necessary to have a sign outside the school saying Durham High School as everyone was just expected to know that the school was there! Marketing has come a long way since then!

'At the time I was working in a tough inner city comprehensive in Newcastle so when I arrived at DHS and walked down the silent corridors, I thought the school must be closed. I was then lulled into thinking that all the girls were as well behaved as the ones I met on the day of my interview!

'Miss Stephenson gave me quite a challenge of a class as my first form – Lower Fourth. They had

Above: Selling wrapping paper in Paris, 1999.

quite a reputation and in my first term at DHS both the class and I were hauled in front of Miss Stephenson as they had more bad comments written by teachers in the termly 'remark' book than all the other classes put together.'

Sage Green Gabardine Coats

'Back in 1986 all the girls had to have a pair of indoor shoes and outdoor shoes so that outdoor shoes didn't make a mess of the carpets in the school! My memories of the uniform at that time were that all the girls, right up to the age of 16, had to wear the school summer dress from May onwards. The design of the dress was not exactly flattering to well-developed young women! The winter uniform at the time was Bainbridge's special sage green dye and the winter coat was a most unflattering sage green gabardine.

'Parents' evenings had the very quaint title of "At Home", which is where I am sure most of the teachers wished they could have been! Thursday

Left: Val Dunsford with her form, 1988.

afternoons were always referred to as the headmistress being "At Home" to parents, which just meant they could make an appointment to see her if they wished.

'Almost every year that I was at the school the Languages department arranged an annual trip to Paris in July for the Lower Fourth (Year 8). We always stayed in a hotel out in the district of Cergy Pontoise and the girls attracted the local youths like bees to a honey pot!'

Fairy Godmothers, a Pumpkin and Mrs Mop
Val Dunsford also recalls: 'We had several staff events to entertain the girls – most notable was the staff pantomime *Cinderella* where Dr Wilkinson (deputy head) played a wonderful Fairy Godmother and a very pregnant Mrs Egglestone was the Pumpkin! The staff fancy dress day brought out some

interesting appearances with Mrs Bell as a high-class tart, Miss Walters as Mrs Mop and myself as Pamela Anderson in her *Baywatch* days!'

Top: Staff, c.1980.

Above: The staff pantomime.

CHAPTER 4

The 1990s to the Present Day

CHAPTER 5

The 1990s to the Present Day

'Training leaders has therefore become an important part of what the school offers.'

Wear and Tear

The six years from 1992 to 1998 with Miss Walters at the helm were a time of rapid change at the school. This was in part a response to national initiatives and increased competition from independent schools in the region. But there was

Above: Miss Walters.

Previous pages: Emily Morris (middle) becomes the millionth person to plant a tree for the Woodland Trust's 'Tree for All' campaign, 2008.

also a realization that the school buildings were insufficient to meet the requirements of a changing and expanding curriculum, especially the rapidly increasing use of information technology.

The buildings were showing signs of wear and tear, in particular there was the need to deal with the constant leaks from the 1960s flat roofs.

Buckets were a familiar sight in various locations in classrooms and corridors. Many Governors' meetings debated whether to spend substantial amounts of money re-roofing specific areas but in the end, although some had to be re-roofed as a matter of urgency, it soon became evident that the only way forward in the long term was to grasp the nettle and plan to rebuild the school – as and when it could be afforded.

This vision, firstly under the chairmanship of Rev. Trounson and subsequently under Mr Bill Hurworth, was the beginning of the impressive rebuilding programme which has accelerated with the construction of splendid new buildings over recent years.

The first major building project – the sixth form block – was judged to be the most pressing need.

Construction (below) and the subsequent opening (below right) of the new sixth form block in 1994.

The sixth form had a classroom on the main corridor next to the school office – the only concession to their senior school status being the provision of a kettle and a sink.

The Numbers Game

'We were all very conscious that, at a time of increased competition between schools and colleges of further education, this was not the best way to attract new pupils or to keep the ones we already had!' Miss Walters said. The new Sixth Form Suite was subsequently opened by retired headmistress Miss Stephenson.

There were major publicity drives to increase the numbers of girls in the school. 'Numbers had decreased with the loss of the little boys in Junior House,' Miss Walters added. This was a time of glossy brochures, flyer sheets, November open days, exhibition stands, new-style advertisements and the development of a distinctive house style.

There was much concentration on management issues in response to innumerable police documents, health and safety regulations as well as personal and social issues. There was also an increased awareness of the need for greater provision for separate sciences at 14+.

Initial plans were drawn up to build new laboratories. At the same time there was an urgent need to modernize provision for the youngest pupils in the school and, after much considered debate, the decision was made that the next building project would be the nursery. Fortunately at the same time the opportunity arose to purchase the adjacent field on South Road, enabling the school to undergo major restructuring and an extension of the car park.

Right: An all girl cast for a nativity play, mid-1990s.

'This could only be done if the old tennis courts were re-sited,' Miss Walters said. 'By then the surface was in very poor condition and there were insufficient courts for the needs of an enthusiastic PE department and expanding extra curricular activities. Space was found at the opposite end of the site and this enabled all three projects to go ahead simultaneously. New laboratories would have to wait until a later date!'

The Rainbow Nursery

In 1987 the school proudly opened The Rainbow Nursery which brought much colour and excitement – along with a bold group of three-year-olds, many of whom have remained with the school and brought us great joy.

From day one our three-year-olds felt at home and grew in confidence and ability with each new day so that the next step into Kindergarten could be taken with ease. A very real sense of community was soon apparent. The Rainbow Nursery was officially opened on 2 October 1997 by Mrs Doreen Hill, who was head of Junior House from 1979 to 1996 and a member of Junior House staff from 1970. It was an afternoon to celebrate a new early beginning to Durham High education.

A recent Ofsted inspection reported that the Rainbow Nursery provided an 'excellent range of purposeful indoor and outdoor activities which provide high levels of challenge'. They considered the children to be 'extremely happy and making outstanding progress' and that 'the quality of teaching and learning is outstanding'.

Boys!

Until 1993, boys attended Junior House from Kindergarten until they went to Prep School at 7½. There were far fewer of them than the girls but they studied alongside quite harmoniously. Sir John Laws (now a judge in the Court of Appeal) well remembers the girls carrying his books for him, and great friendships were struck up. When it came to Nativity plays it was especially useful having the boys for the appropriate roles!

There were adjoining loos outside at the back of Leazes Place and the boys wore grey shorts with

Below: Boys had been a part of the school since the very beginning, but it ceased taking them in 1993, largely due to competition from other local schools. Boys can be seen here enjoying snack time in 1959.

Opposite: Performing Arts Scholars, 2007.

Below: Mrs Templeman.

their school pullovers and ties. Green caps were worn and they were taught to tip them to ladies. Miss Ison particularly loved teaching the boys and made a spirited case for keeping them when it was first mooted they go, which they did not finally do until 1993.

The Last Ten Years

Mrs Templeman joined Durham High School in September 1998 and was the first married headmistress.

At that time there were 424 girls in school. The majority of the senior school girls were clad in thick, beige tights and uniforms which were just beginning to change from sage green to the new bottle green colour.

Black is the New Beige

'Now ten years on with over 600 girls in school, beige tights have long been replaced by black, ties are optional and blazers, now made from a lighter fabric, are worn all day like a jacket,' Mrs Templeman said. 'And new Year 7 girls are to be seen sporting the new green tartan skirt with yellow stripe.'

During these ten years there have been three major building projects – each with memorable opening ceremonies and each reflecting and changing curriculum needs and the growing numbers.

First came the Millennium Building, providing more classrooms for a rapidly expanding Junior House as it became a two form entry school. Matt Baker (of *Blue Peter* fame) opened the building, accompanied by adoring cheers from his young fans.

Next, in 2003, came the Hurworth Building named after the Chairman of Governors, Bill Hurworth, whose vision had made the building possible. It was opened by Olympic Gold Medal athlete Jonathan Edwards, who spoke passionately about the importance of studying science in the light of God's great creative power. The building houses

Left: The Millennium building renamed, on 13 February 2009, The Walters Building after Margaret Walters, Headmistress 1992–8.

Bottom: Jonathan Edwards opens the Hurworth Building in 2003.

Below: Hard at work in the library.

six state of the art science laboratories and provides much-needed facilities for modern study.

This was particularly important for the High School, where at least half of the Sixth Form, which has grown to be over 100 pupils, now study sciences at A level. Many of these pupils go on to read science at university.

Two splendid IT suites are situated downstairs alongside the Schroder Library, the new heart of the school, which Bruno Schroder himself flew in to declare open. The dramatic increase in technology throughout the school, together with the library as a focal point for private study, reflects one of the school's key priorities in the first decade of the twenty-first century – that of fostering independent learning.

A Grand Reunion

An appeal had been launched to raise money for the Hurworth Building. This had not succeeded in raising vast sums of cash but did provide some wonderful opportunities to widen both local and

Below: Lord Templeman and Bruno Schroder, at the Hurworth Building opening, 2003.

Below right: Dr Ruth Etchells in front of the stained glass window she designed for the quiet room.

national interest in the school and contact former pupils. A grand reunion for Old Girls and a reception in the House of Lords, courtesy of Lord Templeman, produced much goodwill, as did a wonderful candlelit dinner at Auckland Castle, at which Old Girl and opera singer Joanna Burton sang magnificently. Joanna's Speech Day address in 2004 was one of the most memorable of the decade. She won girls over immediately with reminiscences of green gym knickers and challenged everyone about the value of the demanding words of the school hymn, *St Patrick's Breastplate*, and inspired us all with her singing.

One of the key features of the new Hurworth Building was the inclusion of a quiet room where girls could be quiet and pray. The centrepiece of the quiet room is a stained glass window designed and made by Dr Ruth Etchells, a former Governor of the High School and former Principal of St John's College. The window is entitled 'A High School Annunciation' and depicts the Virgin Mary wearing Durham High School uniform in the Schroder Library, being called by God to serve Him. The window was dedicated in a special service in the sports hall by the Bishop of Jarrow and Dr Etchells spoke very movingly and powerfully about the meaning of the window and how God calls each individual out of their ordinary, everyday situations, just as he had once called Mary.

Gala Performances

As the Senior School continued to grow, the need for more classrooms became a priority. At the same time the scope and quality of performing arts at the High School increased significantly, thanks partly to the opening of the Gala Theatre in Durham and the invitation to be the first school performing in that professional theatre. The High School production of

Below: Cast member Kirsty Wright performs during the 2008 production of Thoroughly Modern Millie.

Bottom and right: Poster advertising productions performed over the years at the Gala Theatre, Durham.

Bottom right: Cast from The Wizard of Oz.

Our Day Out was performed at the Gala in 2002, and this has been followed each year by a production of ever-increasing ambition and professionalism – *The Lion, The Witch and The Wardrobe, The Sound of Music, Jesus Christ Superstar, The Wizard of Oz, The Secret Garden* and, in 2008, *Thoroughly Modern Millie*. Preparation for such ambitious shows required more space and special facilities for music and drama at school. This demand, together with the need for more classrooms, led to the building of the Salter Block in 2007 containing 16 classrooms with the superb Wendy Craig Performing Arts Suite. The studio contains a stage the same size as the Gala stage, a music technology room and five music practice rooms.

The school was immensely privileged to welcome back Wendy Craig to open the building; undaunted by her taxi failing to arrive on time or her subsequently rushed lunch, she spoke magnificently at the opening ceremony in the sports hall. She then walked smilingly through the line of pupils, reminiscing on the way to the television cameras about her time at the High School before opening the new building, watched by all the school's invited guests including four headmistresses: Miss Salter, Miss Stephenson, Miss Walters and Mrs Templeman. The opening performance, watched in the studio by the invited guests comprised music, dance and drama and Ms Craig responded in kind by speaking of her own acting debut at Durham High School. Also, in 2007 Performing Arts Scholarships were introduced to supplement existing Music Scholarships and other means-tested awards.

Scholarships and Awards

Means-tested awards have been another important development over the last decade. In particular the awards of half fees places by the HSBC and the Ogden Trust, together with similar awards by the

Above: Wendy Craig recollects her days as a pupil at the School.

Left: Opening the Performing Arts Suite that bears her name, 2007.

Right: Girls practise netball after school, 2003.

Far right: Kwik cricket, July 2008.

Bottom right: U14 hockey squad, March 2008.

school, have provided several free places each year. These means-tested scholarships have opened the door to a number of able girls at 11+ and 16+ whose parents could not have possibly afforded the fees. The school community has benefited greatly by widening access in this way and enabling many talented girls to join the school.

From Rounders to Rugby

Another current emphasis is sport. This has always been important and has become increasingly so in the last 10 years as the school has gained the accolade 'of an Academy for Girls' Sport' with funding from Sport England for a multi-skills coach.

The range of sports available to girls has vastly increased. As well as traditional girls' sports of netball, hockey, tennis and rounders girls also have the opportunity to sample the boys territory, namely cricket, rowing, football and rugby as well as more unusual sports like abseiling, golf and salsa dancing. High School girls now compete nationally in many sports including tennis, dry skiing, gymnastics, rowing and eventing.

There is also today a wealth of opportunity simply to have fun at school. Girls can get involved with music workshops, drama, gorge walking, canoeing, rowing, rock climbing, archery, orienteering and gymnastics, as well as endless school trips and expeditions as far afield as Madagascar. The list goes on and on. Miss Gray, our first headmistress, could surely never have imagined the depth of opportunities on offer to today's pupils.

Topping the Leader Board

Alongside the school's rising numbers and expanding facilities, plus improving achievement in performing arts, there has been consistent success in academic standards. William Hurworth, Chair of Governors, said excellence was the schools' goal: 'My lasting memory of Durham High School for Girls will be how it has become one of the best known and respected schools in the North East of England. I have been associated with the School for

Below: Eleanor Gatehouse becoming the cross country north east regional winner in 2007.

Below right: Speech Day, 2004. Mr Hurworth, Chair of Governors, Old Girl, Joanna Burton, who presented the prizes and Mrs Templeman.

over 30 years and, in particular, as Chairman of the Governing Body for 18 of those years. During that time, the School has grown immensely in its structural size and, most importantly, in its educational achievements.'

Each year, since league tables began in the late 1990s, the school has been top of the County and beyond in national league tables and each year a significant number of girls have won places at Oxford, Cambridge and other prestigious universities in subjects ranging from Classics through to Medicine. More important is the fact that almost every girl in the Upper Sixth regularly obtains a place at the university of her choice. This academic success has brought the school onto the national stage, consistently featuring in the *Sunday Times* top 500 independent schools, often the only one in the area, and also the only one in County Durham which has an entry in the prestigious *Good Schools Guide*.

'The key secret of our success is that we are a girls' school; in girls' schools all the physicists, all the computer specialists, all the athletes and all the leaders are girls,' Mrs Templeman says. 'This evident fact provides the necessary confidence to all pupils that they can reach their true potential in every area of the curriculum. Training leaders has therefore become an important part of what the school offers.'

For many years now Durham High School for Girls has produced more girls obtaining Duke of Edinburgh Gold Awards than any other institution in the county and currently there are more than 100 girls working towards their D of E award. Every girl in the Sixth Form undergoes leadership training and undertakes some leadership role within school. The School Council, run by the Head Girl and Deputy

Right: A2 results day, 2007.

Below: Hill walking in the Yorkshire Dales as part of the Duke of Edinburgh Award Scheme. From l–r: Sophie Cronin, Hannah Fulford, Sarah Cook, Stephanie Singh, Sara Vardy.

Opposite: The Schroder Library.

Head Girl, has become an important part of school life in both Junior House and Senior School and has representatives from every year group. They meet regularly to discuss key issues in school.

The Head Girl's story

Alex Gillham joined the school in 1997 and is the current Head Girl (2008): 'Both Sarah (Deputy Head Girl) and I have become quite different people from when we first joined the school, and we feel that our time at Durham High School has definitely helped shape who we are today.

'After attending mixed primary schools, we both began Year 7 at Durham High with nervous excitement about meeting new people and making friends. We soon found that there was no need to worry, however, as the small form groups provided an extremely welcoming atmosphere and meant that we could all bond with each other easily. Despite the comfort of the form groups, most of us felt some shyness towards the other year groups;

I remember feeling that the 13-year-old Year 8s seemed like the oldest, scariest girls I'd ever met. Year 7 was a time when we all began to experiment with our personal style, and we still have the hilarious memories (and embarrassing photos) of the outfits which seemed like a good idea at the time. The experiences of Year 7 generally felt new and exciting, and I try to remember this whenever

Above: Catherine Alabaster, Alex Gillham and Sarah McGuinness.

96

I overhear new girls' enthusiasm about using a microscope, or talking about a weekly test as though it were a life or death situation.

'Years 8 and 9 were confusing times for many of us; while we ourselves felt that we were becoming more mature, with hindsight we can see that we often did not act like the adults we were trying to be! Throughout these two years, every little problem turned into a huge drama, and our friends and I often directed our bad moods towards our parents and each other. However, the "stress" that we invented in Year 9 seemed to disappear in Years 10 and 11. Although these were busy years, with the focus being on GCSEs, we still managed to have a good time with social events both outside and within school. The attitude towards friendship was a lot more relaxed, and many people became a lot

more confident – although we still tried to act a lot older than we were! The end of Year 11 was therefore quite an emotional time, as we said goodbye to some of our friends and realized that after a long summer we'd have to become a lot more independent.

'Although I have always had close friends, throughout my school life I had never really been one of the strongest characters in my year group. With huge encouragement from my teachers and friends, however, I decided to use the opportunities given to me in Sixth Form and I feel that I have the school to thank for my new-found confidence. Sarah has also seized every opportunity to put her interest in drama to good use with her involvement in almost every production. Lower Sixth has therefore been a highlight, as it has allowed us to prepare for adult life without completely throwing us in at the deep end, and even more friendships have been made through sharing a common room with the whole year.

'Although we feel that our personalities and strengths have developed hugely throughout our time at Durham High school, we are thankful for one more year in order to realize our potential as head girl and deputy. It is often funny to see new girls going through similar experiences to our own, and we hope that we can make our last year the best round-off as possible of our time at Durham High School.'

The Hogwarts Factor

The school's priority of growing leaders was one of the key driving forces behind the new emphasis on the House system. A decade ago Houses were mainly concerned with sport but thanks partly to the success of the Harry Potter stories they are again a vital part of all aspects of school life. Our House Captains in the Senior School are part of the new Leadership Team and are expected to create effective teams for all the annual House events including drama, singing and various charity activities as well as the traditional sporting teams. The focus of much of this activity has been the new tradition of St Cuthbert's Day, begun by Mrs Templeman after her sabbatical in Australia. This was partly inspired by constant requests from aspiring sixth form leaders for more 'vertically grouped' activities.

The aim of St Cuthbert's Day, which is a new school tradition, is to have an annual day in the Spring term to celebrate the life of the school and provide opportunities for the girls to work together in Houses for the good of the community – local and global.

A focus on giving

'We named the day St Cuthbert's Day as the St Cuthbert's cross is the school logo and encapsulates the school's priority of Christian service,' Mrs Templeman said.

The first St Cuthbert's Day celebrations took place in March 2007. The Bishop of Jarrow preached at an inspiring service in the sports hall celebrating some key events in the life of the school. The service began with an innovative story with pictures and drama entitled 'Durham High School – This is your Life.' This service was followed by traditional Victorian games in Houses: Easter egg hunts, hopscotch and so on. Next came the House choir competition; each House competed in its entirety with a set song and was judged by visiting governors and guests. The afternoon was then turned over to a charity

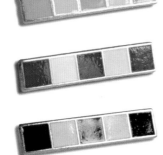

Left: The House badges of Heath, Booth, Neville and Tempest.

Below: House singing, St Cuthbert's Day, 2008.

*Bottom: Bobbing for apples on St Cuthbert's Day, 2008 –
one of the many ways in which the girls raise money for charity.*

fair, with an amazing number of stalls planned in Houses, from dance mats to hair straightening, all in aid of each House charity.

The focus of giving and service has always been a vital part of the life of the High School and underpins all the school stands for. Governors and staff met together in 2000 to discuss and reformulate the aims of the school. They determined that the first aim of the school was to be a community based on Christian values, followed closely by the aim to develop the potential of every girl in every area of her life.

Opposite: Mrs Templeman reads to the children in the newly refurbished Junior Library, 2008.

Our Christian Heritage

Durham High School has always been conscious of its Anglican, Christian heritage; every headmistress has taken seriously the vision of being a church school. In the context of the greater secularization of our society, the school has put greater emphasis on the need to provide opportunities for spiritual growth.

Informal half-termly communion services were started in 1999 and soon afterwards, as a result of pupil demand, Confirmation classes began again. In 2000 the High School returned once again to the cathedral for its annual carol service. This is perhaps one of the most significant initiatives which underlines the Christian heritage and tradition of the school. This wonderful annual service unites all members of the school community – past and present, parents and grandparents, Governors as well as pupils and staff. Every girl who has read or sung

in that awesome building will never forget the privilege and the wonder of worshipping God in that great cathedral.

The former Bishop of Durham, the Rt Rev. Michael Turnbull, vigorously encouraged the emphasis at school on development of spiritual opportunities. As a result, the first full-time lay-chaplain was appointed in 2004. Then in 2005 Mrs Templeman became an ordained deacon and priest.

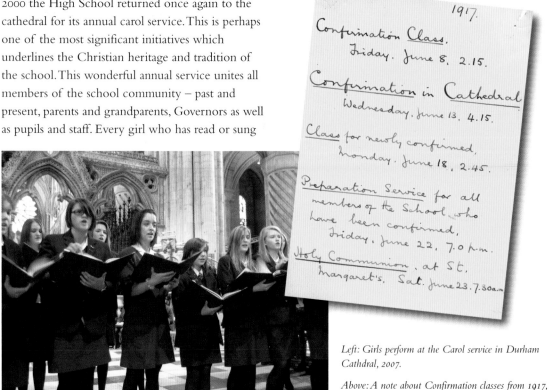

Left: Girls perform at the Carol service in Durham Cathdral, 2007.

Above: A note about Confirmation classes from 1917, containing the order of the day and service information.

Below: Presentation of chalice and paten. From l–r: Jenifer Blair, Eileen Perkins, Mrs Templeman, Ella Wright and the then Bishop of Jarrow (now Bishop of Oxford).

Bottom: The Victorian Fancy Dress Parade.

Mrs Templeman is currently the only female ordained Head of an Anglican school. These developments have made possible numerous other initiatives, notably the growth of voluntary groups of pupils of all ages in school and, in 2007, the introduction of a monthly family service on Sunday afternoons.

Another Birthday

The celebrations for the school's 120th anniversary began on Friday 24 June 2005, postponed from academic year 2004 due to the school inspection.

The Junior School had a celebration assembly which was followed by a visit to Beamish Museum with the staff and pupils in Victorian costume. Meanwhile the Senior School began the day with a Grand Birthday Service in the main school hall attended by the Mayor of Durham, Governors and other invited guests.

The theme of the service was the building of the community. There was drama taking us through some of the history of the school, a humorous sketch on Jesus' parable of the wise man building his house upon the rock and the Bishop of Jarrow spoke to us about building on the foundation stone of Jesus Christ.

After the service there was a school picnic with a number of special house events including a Grand Art Competition, fun sports and face painting. In the evening was our Birthday Ball at the Ramside Hotel, attended by our Upper Sixth leavers and their guests, staff and parents.

The following day we hosted a splendid reunion lunch for a large number of Old Girls. Miss Stephenson, headmistress at the time of the Centenary Celebration attended the event while Ella Wright, head girl at the time of the Jubilee Celebration in 1934, proposed the toast to the

Left: Planting trees for the Woodland Trust's 'Tree for All' campaign .

Below: Skip/Dance Festival, 2008.

school. Fun Day was then formally opened by Old Girl and professional opera singer Joanna Burton. Ably assisted by the Deputy Mayor of Durham, they judged the Fancy Dress Parade of our junior girls dressed in Victorian dress.

It was a really memorable weekend and one that we hope will go down in the archives as one of the great events in the school's history.

In the same year, Dr Ruth Etchells, former principal of St John's College, Durham, unveiled the stained glass window she had created after two years of hard work. The design alone took eight months. At a communion service led by the Bishop of Jarrow and attended by 500 pupils and guests, the window, a chalice donated by the Old Girls' Association, and a paten given by Mrs Ella Wright in memory of her sister were all dedicated.

Below: DHS girls with Mrs Templeman at a church on the visit to Lesotho, 2007.

Bottom right: Visiting communities during the first visit to Lesotho, 2005.

The Link with Lesotho

Our close links with the Diocese of Durham brought about a revived link with the African country of Lesotho. Durham High School had first established connections with St Catherine's School, Lesotho when the link between the Durham and Lesotho diocese was established in 1984. In 2005 the Rev. Rob Bianchi, the Lesotho link officer, welcomed the suggestion that a group of Sixth Form girls from Durham High School should spend some time serving in Lesotho. Since that time groups of about 20 girls and three staff members have spent a month in this AIDS-ravaged country, working especially with AIDS orphans, decorating classrooms and attending HIV peer educators' programmes.

The groups are based at the Link site at the edge of the capital, Maseru, in an accommodation block funded by the generosity of parents and girls at the High School. All who go there find it a life-changing experience. Head Girl Helen Egglestone, who went to Lesotho in 2007, wrote a very moving account about her work in the orphanage:

'Some of us spent a week at an orphanage run by a wonderful lady called M'e Neo. We loved playing with M'e Neo's children, making peg dolls and masks. M'e Neo manages at the moment with no running water and a stinking toilet outside. Without food aid and support from the Link she and her children would starve. Despite this, she and the children are happy and they were so grateful for the gifts we gave them and the time we spent with them. M'e Neo and the children should soon be moving to a new Link-supported centre with bunk

Below: Junior House, winter 2009.

Opposite: Girls from Junior and Senior Houses, making the most of the sunshine, 2008.

beds, showers and toilets. As we said goodbye to M'e Neo I was moved to tears as she said "My prayers go with you, you are all such lovely people". We had been changed by our experiences of poverty and suffering as well as the love and joy we shared with our new friends.'

The Heart of Durham High School
This renewed link has changed the focus of much of school life, putting energy and direction into all charitable giving and service enterprises. Mrs Templeman says: 'For me, one of the most profoundly moving experiences was taking some of our girls to a packed church on the edge of Maseru with a mud floor, tin roof, broken windows and a temperature barely above freezing, and joining in worship with them. Old ladies huddled in colourful blankets on benches, mums decked in the black and grey costumes of the sisters of Mary Magdalene swayed behind them while little children sat, barefoot and squashed together on the floor. We were in the midst of great poverty but at the same time a wonderful life-affirming faith.

'As individuals came up at the end for a blessing and to pray for rain, the congregation sang in Sesotho and danced, swayed, smiled, clapped and blew whistles and gongs and worshipped with their whole hearts. Our girls did their best to join in the words. At the end of the Eucharist our girls made their own contributions by singing with great enthusiasm some of their own favourite hymns. They were welcomed in the traditional Basotho way with a rising crescendo of clapping and

stamping to imitate the coming of rain. That experience was one which will forever remain imprinted on all our memories.'

Twice that year Lesotho television featured the project. Mrs Templeman was able to speak about the joy of sharing together and how much both the Lesotho and English teenagers had learned. During the second TV appearance, the Chairman of the Link, a High Court Lesotho judge, presented the school with a locally-carved plaque containing the Link motto which encapsulated our unforgettable month in that wonderful country: 'We are one body in Christ'.

Mrs Templeman said: 'It is my hope and prayer that the sentiment of unity, harmony and service which underpins that great text, displayed in the foyer for all to see, will always encapsulate the heart of Durham High School for Girls.'

A Family Connection

My grandmother Minnie Louisa Constance Hopkins – as she is listed as Head Girl in 1890 – was the daughter of Randolph Innes-Hopkins of Grimston Manor in Yorkshire. Her school friends at Durham, Jane and Alice Fenwick, were the daughters of Dr James Fenwick (below) of Embleton Hall in Northumberland. The school has a record of Dr Fenwick donating one guinea towards the cost of a tennis court.

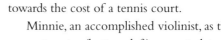

Minnie, an accomplished violinist, as the school's concert poster (bottom left) suggests, later married Ernest Platt of the 13th Somerset Light Infantry. In the early nineteen hundreds, Ernest was sent north as adjutant to the Northumberland Fusiliers and the couple went to live in Northumberland where in 1905 their first son, John, was born. The move gave Minnie the opportunity to renew her friendships. Jane had in the meantime married her distant cousin Lancelot Fenwick of nearby Brinkburn Priory and their first child, Isobel, was born in 1909.

Thirty years on in June 1940, two weeks after Dunkirk from which he had been evacuated, John married Isobel at Brinkburn Priory. Minnie and Alice were present, with Ernest and Lancelot, but sadly Jane had died the year before. I was a son of this marriage.

The picture (top left) shows Jane (seated) with Alice, outside Embleton Hall at about the time they were at the School. The picture of Minnie (left) inscribed 'Mother Oct 1915' is a poignant reminder of the possible lot of talented Durham High School ladies of her age. She presented it as a parting memento to her two sons, aged ten and six. Ernest having been posted to the North West Frontier of India in command of his regiment, she was expected to leave them behind. As the Colonel's wife her duty was to be at his side, and without them, until the war's end – three years on.

Julian Platt
Chairman, Third Millennium Publishing

Head Girls, 1884–2010

April 1884	Geraldine E. Mitton	Sept 1928	Elizabeth Glen	1970–1971	Jill Burton
Jan 1886	Isabel Maud Barnard Headlam	Sept 1930	Edith Mary Leigh	1971–1972	Ruth Vardy
May 1887	Katherine Jane Shields	Sept 1931	Marjorie Treweeke Stokoe	1972–1973	Barbara Atkinson
May 1888	Mary Elizabeth Brown	Sept 1932	Elizabeth Marguerite Ryle	1973–1974	Fiona Andrew
Jan 1889	Annette Barrow Pearce	Sept 1933	Ella W. Costello	1974–1975	Anne Graham
Jan 1890	Frances Rosamund Shields	Sept 1935	Winifred Ryle	1975–1976	Julia Townend
Sept 1890	Minnie Louisa Constance Hopkins	Sept 1937	Rita Gibson	1976–1977	Alison Andrew
Jan 1891	Agnes Rhind	Sept 1938	Beryl Hedley	1977–1978	Linda Smith
Sept 1891	A. Mildred M. Atkinson	Sept 1939	Elizabeth Broadbent	1978–1979	Gillian Holmes
Jan 1892	Gertrude Evelyn Hutton	Sept 1940	Mary Nichol	1979–1980	Amanda Gill
Sept 1892	Ethel Annie Reed	Sept 1941	Eileen Hayton	1980–1981	Rosemary Trigg
Jan 1894	Mary Margaret Pearce	Jan 1942	Marjorie Hetherington	1981–1982	Sandra Pillai
Sept 1894	Mary Alethea Longden	Sept 1943	Margaret Hendry	1982–1983	Claire Hamilton
May 1895	Sarah Taylor	April 1944	Daphne Johnson	1983–1984	Wendy Allen
Jan 1896	Agnes Dorothea Pearce	Sept 1944	Phyllis E. S. Holmes	1984–1985	Donna Larsen
Sept 1897	Catherine Elizabeth Clegg	Sept 1945	Jean M. Calder	1985–1986	Jane Brunskill
Jan 1899	Constance Cartwright Durand	Jan 1946	Ann K. Todd	1986–1987	Andrea Ryan
Jan 1901	Carissima Mary Emma Kendle	1947–1948	Joan Britton	1987–1988	Zelah Senior
Sept 1901	Edith Annie Belshaw	1948–1949	Margaret Todd	1988–1989	Kimberley Riddell
Sept 1902	Edith M. Denholm	1949–1950	Eileen Taylor	1989–1990	Nichola Roberts
Sept 1906	Alice Constance Dawson	1950–1951	Elizabeth Simpson	1990–1991	Jill Wright
May 1907	Mary Dorothea Callinan	1951–1952	Anne Tweddle	1991–1992	Victoria Wheatley
Sept 1908	Dorothy Hunter	1952–1953	Elizabeth Thompson	1992–1993	Victoria Turner
Sept 1909	Mary Frances Tombs	1953–1954	A. Wright, M. Dixon, Angela Monk	1993–1994	Katie Birtwisle
May 1910	Dorothy Nickson	1954–1955	Christine Patullo	1994–1995	Terri Quinn
Sept 1910	Gwendolen Edith Gwyllyam Watkins	1955–1956	Sybil Barker	1995–1996	Claire Epstein
		1956–1957	Valerie Kitching	1996–1997	Naomi Coia
Sept 1911	Dorothy Mary Dodds	1957–1958	Gillian Holmes	1997–1998	Shona Wright
Sept 1913	Lilian Elfrieda Margarethe Mawson	1958–1959	Pamela Armstrong	1998–1999	Rebecca Newlove
		1959–1960	Dorothy Rochester	1999–2000	Elizabeth Ledger
Sept 1915	Eleanor Florence Mary Breguet	1960–1961	Rosemary Martin-Jones	2000–2001	Caroline Beattie
Sept 1916	Dorothy G. Poole	1961–1962	Jennifer Naisbitt	2001–2002	Emma Reilly
Sept 1917	Mary Gwendolen Pearce	1962–1963	Hilary Wetherall	2002–2003	Ingrid E. Frater
Sept 1919	Helena Maud Harrison	1963–1964	June Mallett	2003–2004	Amanda K. Bell
Sept 1920	Dorothy Mary Carpenter	1964–1965	Susan Johnston	2004–2005	Harriet J. Williamson
Sept 1923	Kathleen Honor Nussey Ingham	1965–1966	Ann Stuart	2005–2006	Jenny A. Sneddon
June 1924	Anne R. Stuart	1966–1967	Marjory Robertshaw	2006–2007	Marissa Granath
May 1926	Marjorie H. Gill	1967–1968	Stephanie Bramwell	2007–2008	Helen Egglestone
May 1927	Catherine Mary Nussey Ingham	1968–1969	Fiona McKinnon	2008–2009	Alex Gillham
Jan 1928	Nora Iris Cook	1969–1970	Sarah Jamison	2009–2010	Jennifer Baker

List of Subscribers

This book has been made possible through the generosity of the following subscribers:

Susan and Natasha Abbott
Hayley Anderson
Katherine Anderson
Janet Ash
Shanaya Zahi Atkinson-Jones
Imogen Rose Austin
Amy Baird
Charlotte Anne Baker
Jennifer Rose Baker
Sophie Antonia Barclay Erdmann
Catherine Bartlett
Rachel Beekman
Jenifer Blair
Gerald Blake
Anne Breeze (née Thornton)
Philippa Breeze
Alison Brooks-Shea
M. Brown
Sheila Bryce
Patricia, Joanna and Penelope Burton
Chantalle Carden
Amy Cartwright
Emma Cartwright
Karen Cave (née Williams)
Naomi, Chelsea, Paige and
    Robyn Challans
Stephen J.G. Cheffings
Sonia M. Christie

Naomi Clement
Sarah Connell
N. Pamela Cooke (née Wood)
Victoria Cottier
Angela Craggs
Megan and Rosie Craggs
Miss Wendy Craig
Molly Cronin
Susan C. Crowther (née Morrison)
Morag Cummings (née Laws)
Sarah Suzanne Davie
Alice Dixon
Harriet Dixon
Laura Dunn
Jane Dunn
Mrs Valerie Dunsford
Sue Ellis (née Hicks)
Susan Ellis
Erin Ellwood
Helen English (née Hughes)
Dr Ruth Etchells
Grace Victoria Evans
Judith Evans (née Staddon)
Mary Fairbairn (née Hall)
Elenore Lawson Falshaw
Jean M. Ferguson
Elle Darci-Anne Forbes
Moira Frost

Chloé Fulton
Eleanor Gatehouse
Samantha Jayne Gibson
Anne-Marie Gillbanks
Anna Louise Golightly
Kate Emma Golightly
Claire Gorman (née Taylor)
Katie Gorman
Jean Graham (née Macdonald)
Annabel Gray
Ann Gray (née McColl)
Philippa Gray
Hannah Gregory
Sarah Gregory
Stephen Hall
Holly Hamilton
Matilda Hamilton
Rachel E. Hamilton
Anna Camilla Jane Hankey
Lucille Kay Hankey (née Makin)
Elspeth Harland (née Sterling)
Jennifer Hart
Imogen Heywood
Ursula Heywood
M.A. Hill
Miss J.L. Hobbs MBE
Barbara Hodgson (née Middlemiss)
Elizabeth Holdsworth (née Newton)

Carolyn Hopper (née Raine)

The Hopps Family

Alison House

Catherine Diana Howell (née Mines)

Louise Hume

Laura E. Hunter

William Hurworth

Alice Jackson

Caroline Jackson

Elizabeth Jackson

Fiona Jackson

Sarah Jackson

Paula Jefferson

Marilyn Jeffes (Sievers)

Christine Jennings

Jane Jewitt

Margaret Johnson (née Ashurst)

Heather M. Johnston

Jill Kee (née Burton)

Sarah and Ellen Kerry

Mrs D. Kobasa

Erica May Lamb

Mary Kenny Lascelles (née Fitzpatrick)

Sarah Beatrice Mary Clare Lascelles

Jane Liow

Jennifer Clare Litherland

Evangeline Long

Mrs Ann F. Lowe (née Rainbow)

Michael Maddison

Rosemary Martin-Jones

Beth Masterman

Sarah McGuinness

Barbara McKinnon

Judy Miller

Elizabeth R. Morgan

Fiona Morrall

Jacqueline Murray

Emma Louise Nicholson

Libby-Isla Nicholson

Olivia-Kate Nicholson

Lisa Nyström (née Bhattacharya)

Sarah Jane Osborne

Jane Owens (née Hamilton)

Judith Owens (née Routledge)

J. Carol Parker (née Robinson)

Phoebe Parker

Lara Jane Patel

Chantal Peacock

Helen Olive Peacock

Eileen Perkins (Hankey)

Mrs M. Perreur-Lloyd

Diana Phillips

Jacqueline Phillips

Dr Janet Porter (née Sterling)

Mrs Gill Prescott

Zoe Pulman

Pamela Redpath (née Armstrong)

June Riddell (née Mallett)

Linda Riddle

Mrs K. Roberts

Lucy Jane Roberts

Charlotte Louise Robinson

Hannah Jayne Robinson

Helen Louise Robson

Margaret G. Robson

Winifred Robson

Emma Claire Roebuck (née Hankey)

Margaret Mary Rogers (née Hardy)

Judith O Sample (née Taylor)

Lily Sanderson

Phoebe Sanderson

Cornelia Schwab

Juliana Schwab

Alexandra Kate Sigley (née Hankey)

Dorothy Sills

Marjory Soar (née Robertshaw)

Sophie Sobo

Stephanie Ann Spiers

Kathlyn Standring (née Joyce)

G.H. Steel

Miss B.E. Stephenson

Lucy Stewart

Becky Taylor

Jane Taylor (née Minto)

Patricia Taylor

Ann Templeman

Lord Templeman

Margery Thompson (née Watson)

Sasha and Sienna Thompson

Amanda Thornton

Joan Thornton (née Smith)

Miss Kate Tomlinson

Christine Turnbull (née Bullick)

Dr Susan Turnbull (née Dent)

Elizabeth and Emma (née Vardy)

Chloe Beth Walker

Pat Walker

Miss M.L. Walters

Kathryn M. Waters

Alice Webster

Dr Margaret Wilkinson

Megan and Holly Williams

Mrs Joyce Williams

Hannah and Sophie Wilson

Sheila Wilson (née Reay)

Fiona Elizabeth Wood

Faye Victoria Wood

Bridget Wright

Clare Wright

Shona Wright

Dr Jane Young (née Powell)

Nicola Young

Index of Names

Acknowledgements

The editor and the publishers would like to thank the following people for their assistance in putting this book together:

Kath Anderson, Jenifer Blair, Helen Egglestone, Susan Egglestone, Dr Ruth Etchells, Alex Gillham, Monica Hayton, Sir John Laws, John Neeson, Barbara Stephenson, the late Joan Trowbridge (compiler of the Centenary Booklet), Margaret Walters, Dr Wilkinson (Deputy Head of Durham High School, 1984–90, who wrote the historical note for the Centenary Booklet) and Ella Wright.

We would also wish to thank the members of the DHS History Club: Hayley Bradley, Jennifer Beirne-Oliver, Emma Callaghan, Jessica England, Miss K. Jackson, Emily Patterson, Phoebe Shore, Caitlin Slowther, Beth Smith, Hannah Whittaker and Olivia Wood.

Special thanks also goes to Jacqui Durcan for her invaluable knowledge and extensive time in sourcing material for the book.

Photo credits:
©Corbis, 78; M. Haighton, 68; John Catt Educational Ltd, Saxmundham, 79; *Northern Echo*, 62–3, 64; Severn House Publishing (*The Foxglove Tree* cover), 52; *Sunderland Echo*, 60; *The* Journal 82–3, 102; Walton Adams Photography, 72–3; Westminster Press Ltd, 44–5, 69;